'Anglophones of the next century will be deeply in [Dr Screech's] debt' – Gore Vidal in the *Times Literary Supplement*

'Screech's fine version . . . must surely serve as the definitive English Montaigne.' – A.C. Grayling

Michel Eyquem de Montaigne was born in 1533, the eldest child of a family that owned estates near Bordeaux. Object of a pedagogical experiment that saw him spending early infancy with a peasant family, then learning Latin as his mother tongue, Montaigne trained and practiced as a lawyer in Bordeaux and from 1561–3 was counsellor to the court of Charles IX, just as the religious conflict between the Calvinist Huguenots and the conservative Catholic league was growing intense. Distressed by the death of his close friend Étienne de la Boétie in 1563, and troubled by the sectarian wars, in 1571 Montaigne withdrew to his family estates where, over twenty years – interrupted only by a spell as Mayor of Bordeaux – he put together 1,300 pages of reflections, or *essais*, that constitute one of the most extraordinary bodies of thought in European history.

Born in Manchester in 1954, Tim Parks moved to Italy in 1981. Author of four bestselling books on Italy and fifteen novels, including the Booker shortlisted *Europa*, he has translated works by Moravia, Calvino, Calasso, Machiavelli and Leopardi. While running a postgraduate degree course in translation at IULM University, Milan, he writes regularly for the *LRB* and the *NYRB*. His non-fiction works include *Translating Style*, a literary approach to translation problems, and most recently *Where I'm Reading From*, a collection of short essays.

Michel de Montaigne

–

DRAWN FROM LIFE

–

Translated by M. A. Screech

with an introduction by

Tim Parks

Notting Hill Editions

Published in 2016
by Notting Hill Editions Ltd
Widworthy Barton Honiton Devon EX14 9JS

Designed by FLOK Design, Berlin, Germany
Typeset by CB editions, London

Printed and bound
by Memminger MedienCentrum, Memmingen, Germany

Essays selected from *The Complete Essays* first published by Allen Lane
The Penguin Press 1991

Frontispiece: Michel de Montaigne, copyright Georgios Kollidas

A CIP record for this book
is available from the British Library

ISBN 978-1-910749-23-4

www.nottinghilleditions.com

.

Contents

Tim Parks

– Introduction –

Remarking on a painter he had hired to decorate his house, a man whose habit was to fill in the empty spaces around his central painting with 'odd fantastic figures without any grace but what they derive from their variety,' Montaigne draws a comparison with his own writing, 'And in truth,' he says, 'what are these things I scribble, if not grotesques and monstrous bodies, made of various parts, without any certain figure, or any other than accidental order, coherence, or proportion?'

By way of corroboration, he tosses in a line from the Roman poet Horace, *Desinit in piscem mulier formosa superne* ('a fair woman in her upper form ends in a fish'), then winds up observing that while at least the painter begins with a strong, clear picture and only adds the grotesques around as fillers, he alas, as a writer, is incapable of providing 'a rich piece, finely polished, and set off according to art'. Only the grotesques.

Does he mean it? Is this a promising way to speak of a collection of essays that in its unabridged version runs to 1,300 pages? Grotesques, without any other than 'accidental order'?

Montaigne, the novelist Thackeray wryly observed,

could have switched the titles of all his essays around for all the difference it would have made; the content was always the same. 'Montaigne is a fog,' pronounced T. S. Eliot, 'a gas, a fluid, insidious element. He does not reason, he insinuates.' Montaigne 'has truly increased the joy of living on this earth,' enthuses Nietzsche. He was 'the freest and mightiest of souls'.

How disorienting. Perhaps our puzzlement approaching Montaigne is that while on the one hand we immediately feel drawn into a relationship and recognise the warmth of an intimate voice, something we tend to equate with modernity, on the other we have no idea where that voice is going or why. What is this all *about*? And what could be less modern than stringing together dozens, scores, literally hundreds of quotations from the authors of Roman antiquity? (*Mihi sic usus est: tibi, ut opus est facto, face*, he cites the playwright Terence, shortly after giving us Horace's mermaid – 'This has been my way; as for you, do whatever you find appropriate'). Montaigne seems familiar, sometimes too familiar – he appears to know and understand our inner lives – yet remains quite exotic, as if he inhabited a parallel world whose basic coordinates were obscure to us.

Whenever a new acquaintance is both bewitching and bewildering, it's as well to check out their background. How does or did this behaviour fit in with the society that produced it? Was it normal perhaps? Or at least in evident opposition to the norms of the time?

Michel Eyquem de Montaigne was born in 1533 on his family's estate Chateau de Montaigne, some thirty-five miles east of Bordeaux, and his infancy was anything but normal. First surviving child of wealthy parents, he was installed with a peasant family for the first three years of his life, because he must get to know the common people, then brought home, but given a German tutor who didn't know French and was instructed to speak to him only in Latin. Everybody who spoke to the boy was to speak in Latin, never French, until he was six. It was to be his mother tongue. After which he was dispatched to a posh college in Bordeaux to study law.

In short, Montaigne was the product of an educational experiment at a time when those who could afford such things had become fascinated by the possibilities of social and psychological engineering. Like all educational experiments it produced something, or someone, quite different from what was intended. Diligent and industrious, with a steadfast dedication to public duty displayed both as a soldier in Italy and as Mayor of Bordeaux, Montaigne's father was dismayed to find his son disorganised, impractical and inclined to take things easy. A first will, later revoked, gave control of the family estate to his wife – something quite unusual at the time – for fear the boy, then a teenager, wouldn't perform.

For his part Michel was dismayed to see his father worn out by his commitment to civic duties and later afflicted by excruciating bladder stone pains. The son's whole life might be seen as a demonstration for educators of the impossibility of shaping another's character and destiny according to a predetermined model. That he nevertheless loved and admired his father and insisted that his education was the best a child could ever have, only added to the benevolent irony that seeps through all Montaigne's thinking; it was the right education because it did not produce what its designer intended.

'What is it that makes all our quarrels end in death nowadays?' asks Montaigne in one of the essays in this book, and in so doing points to another circumstance that profoundly affected his approach to life. Violence. Aged fifteen, at college in Bordeaux, he was witness to street riots and saw the governor of the town beaten to death. At home his father entertained the family with terrifying accounts of military butchery in Italy. Above all, there were the so-called 'religious wars' between Catholics and Protestants that kept France in a state of civil strife more or less continuously from 1562 through to the end of the century. Pitching one Christian dogmatism against another, nobles against king, dynasty against dynasty and state against state, the wars were as cruel as they were complex, leading to hundreds of thousands of deaths, in mob massacres, open warfare, executions and assassinations. 'In our time above all', Montaigne remarks, 'you cannot talk to the world in general except dangerously or falsely.' At no point in his essays does he discuss the doctrinal or even political differences between the two sides. It was the only way to avoid danger and falsity. Yet the endless 'odd fantastic figures' he conjures up for us constantly imply that missing scene of violence in their centre, its peril and its folly.

What was it, though, that made these quarrels end in death? The essay that puts that question is entitled 'On Cowardice, the Mother of Cruelty' and begins rather oddly by attributing people's haste to kill to their cowardice; if they really wanted revenge they would make sure their enemies stayed alive to savour their defeat ('To kill a man is to shield him from our attack'). By the end of the essay, however, he is making what might seem the opposite reflection, that 'Everything which goes beyond mere death [i.e. torture] seems to me to be cruelty.' And this again is the product of cowardice. Both killing and causing gratuitous suffering are cowardly. The drift beneath the surface, never openly stated, no doubt for fear of religious dogmatism, is that flexibility and clemency are the only real courage. 'Souls are most beautiful when they show most variety and flexibility,' he tells us in another essay discussing quite other matters. 'We should not nail ourselves so strongly to our humours and complexions.'

So if a certain mild waywardness was Montaigne's reaction to his father's educational regime, a refusal to engage passionately with doctrinal differences was his response to the religious wars. He is Catholic, he tells us, but has great respect for the Protestants. The word 'Christian' only occurs once in this selection, thus: 'When we hear our Christian martyrs shouting out to the tyrant from the midst of the flames, "It is well roasted on this side; chop it off and eat it; it is cooked just right: now start on the other side [. . .]" then we have to admit that there is some change for the worse in their souls, some frenzy, no matter how holy.' Where I have shown an elision Montaigne inserts a similar but non-Christian example of fanatic martyrdom that runs to a full ten lines, thus keeping the words 'Christian' and 'frenzy' safely apart.

Aside from the threat of war and violence – at nineteen Montaigne was present at the siege of prot-estant Rouen, in his fifties he would be captured by bandits and briefly imprisoned in the Bastille – there was the ever present hazard of disease and early death. Outbreaks of the plague occurred in Bordeaux in 1548, 1563, 1585 and 1586. Infant mortality was the norm. Montaigne's parents had lost two children be-fore him and he and his wife would lose five of the six children born to them in early infancy. In 1563, aged thirty, Montaigne lost the one great passion of his life to the plague. A man not a woman. There were women and, he admits, doses of the clap – no pleasure without danger – but the one truly intense friendship of his life was with fellow lawyer Étienne de La Boétie. It was a meeting of minds and dispositions that had nothing to do with any shared cause or creed, a friendship entirely focused on mutual regard, lasting just five years, much of the time being spent apart. Later, Montaigne would write that relationships must never become so close that they cannot be lost 'without flaying us or tearing out part of our whole'. Rather 'we must espouse nothing but ourselves'. It was a strategy for survival.

Whether talking about death in war or from sickness, Montaigne's reflections on mortality – and almost everything he speaks about brings him back to that – are always framed in terms of fear and courage. However much he digresses, backtracks or meanders, this is the force field in which experience is understood. Fear is the most understandable reaction in the world, since the world is unspeakably dangerous. But it robs us of ourselves. In battle, sports, or sex, it prevents us from performing (Montaigne has a great deal to say about impotence). Fear inhibits freedom and freedom, which requires constant courage, remains the supreme good. 'I am so sick for freedom that if anyone should forbid me access to some corner of the Indies I should live distinctly less comfortably.' When he tells us that 'the thing in the world I am most afraid of is fear', it is because the fearful man has lost his freedom. A courtier cannot be free, because constant concerns over his master's reaction 'corrupt his freedom and dazzle him'. When Montaigne attacks social customs it is because they inhibit his freedom; afraid of breaking with tradition one is frustrated and constrained. 'Whichever way I want to go I find myself obliged to break through some barrier of custom,' he opens an essay entitled 'The Custom of Wearing Clothing'. The endless examples he gives of outlandishly different traditions in different times and climes are all quietly aimed at eroding the intimidating pressure of present custom.

How to be free, then, and enjoy life in a world that demands so much of us? On his thirty-eighth birthday, six years after Étienne de la Boétie's death and shortly after a near-death experience of his own following a collision on horseback, Montaigne had these words painted on a wall in his home:

In the year of Christ 1571 . . . Michel de Montaigne, long weary of the servitude of the court and of public employments, while still entire retired to the bosom of the learned Virgins, where in calm and freedom from all cares he will spend what little remains of his life now more than half run out.

Retirement. Shun obligation. Shun passion. Once you are in something, it is hard to get out. 'I find that the remedy which works for me is, from the outset, to purchase my freedom at the cheapest price I can get . . . With very little effort I stop the first movement of my emotions, giving up whatever begins to weigh on me before it bears me off.' In his house, all customary etiquette was waived; family members were not obliged to exchange tedious pleasantries. Murals of famous battles and ships in stormy seas reminded Montaigne of the dangers he had renounced. Meantime, he retired to the little tower where he kept his library; one great advantage of the relationships we have with books, he remarks, is that they aren't upset when you put them down for a while. Alone in his room, he waited for the learned Virgins, the muses, to show him what to write.

It would not be a grand treatise or an all-encompassing system of thought; for, alongside social obligation, ambition with its consequent fear of under-achievement, was another dangerous enemy. One had to have courage to underachieve. Even philosophy, in excess, will 'enslave our natural freedom'; even attacking custom could become an imprisoning hobby horse. Fortunately, friends in his younger days 'judging rightly enough of my own strength that it was not capable of any great matters' had encouraged him 'to free myself from any such ambition, and to sit still'.

So Montaigne sat still and wrote. Or rather he paced back and forth, or went out for walks, because when he sat too long the thoughts would not flow. Wrote what? 'I would have preferred to publish my whimsies as letters,' he said, 'if I had had anyone to write to.' Anyone, that is, on the same wavelength, like La Boétie. Why letters? Because they offered oppor-tunities for intimacy, for acknowledging subjectivity, tying what was said to the mood of the moment. And of course for dialogue, which is the enemy of all dogma-tism and a means of turning enquiry into pleasure. Ad-mirers of Montaigne make large claims about the essay form he was to develop in the absence of a suitable correspondent. Sarah Bakewell, for example, believes that he single-handedly created a peculiarly autobiographical form of writing. This is not quite true; his models go right back to Plato and Cicero. 'You will probably detect my inner restlessness in the changeable behaviour in my letters,' Cicero writes. That is exactly the tone Montaigne was looking for. Closer to his time, from Petrarch onward the Italian Renaissance was full of writers looking for a more intimate tone in which to frame their reflections. Montaigne read them avidly. In France, a friend of his, Étienne Pasquier, published a collection of letters which he referred to as a 'history of my inclinations'. It would not have been a bad title for Montaigne's essays.

Nevertheless, as he began to work in this tradition, Montaigne did indeed transform it into something quite new, an irresistible mix of purposefulness and digression, purposefulness *in* digression, and above all juxtaposition. His extraordinary knowledge of Roman literature, by-product of his father's educational scheming, was crucial. The authors of antiquity offered a vast store of respectable anecdote spread across many centuries and far-flung lands. Whatever subject Montaigne tackled, he could summon any number of colourful examples to his aid. Publius Sulpicius Galba did this. The philosopher Solon said that. King Massinissa could not be persuaded to wear anything on his head, come cold, wind or rain. According to Suetonius. The same is said of Hannibal. Certain Cythian women could kill their enemies just by looking at them. Pythagoras's daughter-in-law thought a woman 'should doff her modesty with her kirtle'. Certain Brahmin virgins, being ugly, would put their 'matrimonial parts' on display to attract a husband. Pliny says bladder stones are a good reason for suicide. Emperor Theophilus was so amazed to find himself losing a battle against the Agarenes, he couldn't even run away. And so on.

Presented without any geographical or chronological context, these narrative fragments create the impression of a hugely variegated, ongoing body of human experience where simply anything is possible. The effect is reinforced by mixing modern history with ancient, yesterday's news from Paris with bizarre tribal behaviour in the Americas; the public rubs elbows with the personal, myth with history, the solemn with the trivial. In the process, each string of anecdotes risks becoming more interesting and piquant than the general argument it was supposed to be supporting. Talking about the power of the imagination to affect the body, we shift from Latin poetry evoking adolescent wet dreams, to Gallus Vibius who tried so hard to empathise with the mad that he became mad himself, to girls who thought so much about the male member that they developed one, to saints and their stigmata, and, out of the blue, a long discussion on the psychosomatic basis of impotence. A hilarious personal anecdote is followed by 'Amasis, a King of Egypt' who 'wed

Laodice, a very beautiful Grecian maiden' but, finding himself unable to perform in bed, suspected her of witchcraft. This anecdote then gives way to some sound advice for dealing with impotence in married life and casual sexual encounters. 'Those who know that their member is naturally obedient should merely take care to out-trick their mental apprehensions.'

'The stubborn nature of my stones, especially when in my prick . . .' begins one paragraph in another essay, again apparently apropos of nothing. It was the kind of intimate confession that many readers, particularly in more priggish times, would find hard to understand or forgive. Yet considering the overall effect of the essays, it's clear that these moments of scabrous personal revelation are an essential part of his underlying strategy. Montaigne is at pains (to risk a pun) to remind us how much we are at the whim of our bodies, so many parts of which have lives of their own. 'Our members have emotions proper to themselves which arouse them or quieten them down without leave from us.' Even our will can be 'charged with sedition and rebellion because of its unruliness and disobedience. Does it always wish what we want it to?' We are bundles of absurd contradictions without any continuity. Hence, implicitly, any pretense of laying down severe doctrines is absurd.

This was another thing that later readers of Montaigne were to find alarming: the apparent lack of any hard core of belief, any public-spirited advice. Blaise

Pascal in particular, a man who began as a scientist and became a fervent Christian apologist, who twined together that is, the two main strands of intellectual life in the 17th century, was fascinated and appalled by Montaigne. 'He contradicts both those who maintain that all is uncertainty, and those who maintain it not, because he does not want to maintain anything at all.' How could science thrive if a mentality like this took hold? How could religion thrive?

Pascal's opposition to Montaigne, condescendingly laughed off by Montaigne enthusiasts, alerts us to the abyss between mainstream Western thought and the spirit of these essays. They are so engaging, so seductive, that many readers will revel in their intimacy and irreverence without entirely grasping the challenge they throw down to us. Thirsting for freedom in the deepest sense, Montaigne, like the Buddha so many centuries before him, identifies his enemy in our attachment to the world and its pleasures, our inability to let go. It is this that enslaves us. Life, he concluded, was to be enjoyed or suffered moment by moment, without seeking to control or direct it overall.

When I dance, I dance; when I sleep, I sleep. Nay, when I walk alone in a beautiful orchard, if my thoughts are some part of the time taken up with external occurrences, I some part of the time call them back again to my walk, to the orchard, to the sweetness of that solitude, and to myself.

Life, like each essay, is a performance, happening now. If I digress, I digress.

Pascal on the contrary thirsted not for freedom, but for meaning, for explanations and revelations, scientific and religious. One lived in preparation for the future, in a spirit of progress, and expectation of the afterlife, seeking to understand and control. Pascal's position – but it is also Galileo's and Bacon's and Newton's – would be absolutely victorious, it is our inheritance. Montaigne suggests a way that Western thought might still have taken, not based on information, idealism or concepts of progress. He is perhaps the last writer who gathers together the vast wisdom of antiquity and, entirely ignoring Christianity, seeks to seduce us toward a happier way of life. The Vatican knew exactly what it was doing when it included the Essays in its index of banned books from 1674 to 1858.

Not that Montaigne thought one should withdraw entirely from the world. In 1582, having published a first volume of essays and already suffering from the bladder stones that had plagued his father and would kill him ten years later, Montaigne was invited, almost ordered, to become Mayor of Bordeaux. Reluctantly, he accepted, but laid down his terms: he was willing to take public duties 'in hand' but 'not in lung nor in liver! I accept the burdens but I refuse to make them parts of my body.' In short, he would not make himself ill. 'He who does not live a little for others hardly lives at all for himself' but 'any man who gives up a sane and happy life in order to provide one for others makes (in my opinion) a bad and unnatural decision.'

That parenthesis '(in my opinion)', with its implicit recognition that his views are there to be taken or left, not imposed, conceals all the man's discreet and beguiling genius.

TO THE READER

You have here, Reader, a book whose faith can be trusted, a book which warns you from the start that I have set myself no other end but a private family one. I have not been concerned to serve you nor my reputation: my powers are inadequate for such a design. I have dedicated this book to the private benefit of my friends and kinsmen so that, having lost me (as they must do soon) they can find here again some traits of my character and of my humours. They will thus keep their knowledge of me more full, more alive. If my design had been to seek the favour of the world I would have decked myself out better and presented myself in a studied gait. Here I want to be seen in my simple, natural, everyday fashion, without striving or artifice: for it is my own self that I am painting. Here, drawn from life, you will read of my defects and my native form so far as respect for social convention allows: for had I found myself among those peoples who are said still to live under the sweet liberty of Nature's primal laws, I can assure you that I would most willingly have portrayed myself whole, and wholly naked.

And therefore, Reader, I myself am the subject of my book: it is not reasonable that you should employ your leisure on a topic so frivolous and so vain.

Therefore, Farewell:

From Montaigne;
this first of March, One thousand, five hundred and eighty.

– We Reach the Same End
by Discrepant Means –

T he most common way of softening the hearts
of those we have offended once they have us at
their mercy with vengeance at hand is to move them to
commiseration and pity by our submissiveness. Yet flat
contrary means, bravery and steadfastness, have sometimes served to produce the same effect.

Edward, Prince of Wales – the one who long governed our Guyenne and whose qualities and fortune
showed many noteworthy characteristics of greatness
– having been offended by the inhabitants of Limoges,
took their town by force. The lamentations of the
townsfolk, the women and the children left behind
to be butchered crying for mercy and throwing themselves at his feet, did not stop him until eventually,
passing ever deeper into the town, he noticed three
French noblemen who, alone, with unbelievable bravery, were resisting the thrust of his victorious army.
Deference and respect for such remarkable valour first
blunted the edge of his anger; then starting with those
three he showed mercy on all the other inhabitants of
the town.

Scanderbeg, Prince of Epirus, was pursuing one
of his soldiers in order to kill him. The soldier, having

assayed all kinds of submissiveness and supplications to try and appease him, as a last resort resolved to await him, sword in hand. Such resolution stopped his Master's fury short; having seen him take so honourable a decision he granted him his pardon. (This example will allow of a different interpretation only from those who have not read of the prodigious strength and courage of that Prince.)

The Emperor Conrad III had besieged Guelph, Duke of Bavaria; no matter how base and cowardly were the satisfactions offered him, the most generous condition he would vouchsafe was to allow the noblewomen who had been besieged with the Duke to come out honourably on foot, together with whatever they could carry on their persons. They, with greatness of heart, decided to carry out on their shoulders their husbands, their children and the Duke himself. The Emperor took such great pleasure at seeing the nobility of their minds that he wept for joy and quenched all the bitterness of that mortal deadly hatred he had harboured against the Duke; from then on he treated him and his family kindly.

Both of these means would have swayed me easily, for I have a marvellous weakness towards mercy and clemency – so much so that I would be more naturally moved by compassion than by respect. Yet for the Stoics pity is a vicious emotion: they want us to succour the afflicted but not to give way and commiserate with them.

Now these examples seem to me to be even more to the point in that souls which have been assaulted and assayed by both those methods can be seen to resist one without flinching only to bow to the other.

It could be said that for one's mind to yield to pity is an effect of affability, gentleness – and softness (that is why weaker natures such as those of women, children and the common-people are more subject to them) – whereas, disdaining tears and supplications and then yielding only out of respect for the holy image of valour is the action of a strong, unbending soul, reserving its good-will and honour for stubborn, masculine vigour. Yet ecstatic admiration and amazement can produce a similar effect in the less magnanimous. Witness the citizens of Thebes: they had impeached their captains on capital charges for having extended their mandates beyond the period they had prescribed and preordained for them; they were scarcely able to pardon Pelopidas, who, bending beneath the weight of such accusations, used only petitions and supplications in his defence, whereas on the contrary when Epaminondas came and gloriously related the deeds he had done and reproached the people with them proudly and arrogantly, they had no heart for even taking the ballots into their hands: the meeting broke up, greatly praising the high-mindedness of that great figure.

The elder Dionysius had captured, after long delays and extreme difficulties, the town of Rhegium together with its commander Phyton, an outstanding man who had stubbornly defended it. He resolved to make him into a terrible example of vengeance. Dionysius first told him how he had, the previous day, drowned his son and all his relations. Phyton merely replied that they were happier than he was, by one day. Next he had him stripped, seized by executioners and dragged through the town while he was flogged, cruelly and ignominiously, and plied with harsh and shameful insults. But Phyton's heart remained steadfast and he did not give way; on the contrary, with his face set firm he loudly recalled the honourable and glorious cause of his being condemned to death – his refusal to surrender his country into the hands of a tyrant – and he threatened Dionysius with swift punishment from the gods. Dionysius read in the eyes of the mass of his soldiers that, instead of being provoked by the taunts which this vanquished enemy made at the expense of their leader and of his triumph, they were thunder-struck by so rare a valour, beginning to soften, wondering whether to mutiny, and ready to snatch Phyton from the hands of his guards; so he brought Phyton's martyrdom to an end and secretly sent him to be drowned in the sea.

Man is indeed an object miraculously vain, various and wavering. It is difficult to found a judgement on him which is steady and uniform. Here you have Pompey pardoning the entire city of the Mamertines, against whom he was deeply incensed, out of consideration for the valour and great-heartedness of Zeno, a citizen who assumed full responsibility for the public wrong-doing and who begged no other favour than alone to bear the punishment for it. Yet that host of Sylla showed similar bravery in the city of Perugia and gained nothing thereby, neither for himself nor for the others.

And, directly against my first examples, Alexander, the staunchest of men and the most generous towards the vanquished, stormed, after great hardship, the town of Gaza and came across Betis who commanded it; of his valour during the siege he had witnessed staggering proofs; now Betis was alone, deserted by his own men, his weapons shattered; all covered with blood and wounds, he was still fighting in the midst of several Macedonians who were slashing at him on every side. Alexander was irritated by so dearly won a victory (among other losses he had received two fresh wounds in his own body); he said to him: 'You shall not die as you want to, Betis! Take note that you will have to suffer every kind of torture which can be thought up against a prisoner!' To these menaces Betis (not only looking assured but contemptuous and proud) replied not a word. Then Alexander, seeing his haughty and stubborn silence said: 'Has he bent his knee? Has he let a word of entreaty slip out? Truly I will overcome that refusal of yours to utter a sound: if I cannot wrench a word from you I will at least wrench a groan.' And as his anger turned to fury he ordered his heels to be pierced and, dragging him alive behind a cart, had him lacerated and dismembered.

Was it because bravery was so usual for him that he was never struck with wonder by it and therefore respected it less? Or was it because he thought bravery to be so properly his own that he could not bear to see it at such a height in anyone else without anger arising from an emotion of envy; or did the natural violence of his anger allow of no opposition? Truly if his anger could ever have suffered a bridle it is to be believed that it would have done so during the storming and sack of Thebes, at seeing so many valiant men put to the sword, men lost and with no further means of collective defence. For a good six thousand of them were killed, none of whom was seen to run away or to beg for mercy; on the contrary all were seeking, here and there about the streets, to confront the victorious enemy and to provoke them into giving them an honourable death. None was so overcome with wounds that he did not assay with his latest breath to wreak revenge and to find consolation for his own death in the death of an enemy. Yet their afflicted valour evoked no pity; a day was not long enough to slake the vengeance of Alexander: this carnage lasted until the very last drop of blood remained to be spilt; it spared only those who were disarmed – the old men, women and children – from whom were drawn thirty thousand slaves.

– On Fear –

Obstupui, steteruntque comae, et vox faucibus haesit.
[I stood dumb with fear; my hair stood on end and my voice
stuck in my throat.]

I am not much of a 'natural philosopher' – that is the term they use; I have hardly any idea of the mechanisms by which fear operates in us; but it is a very odd emotion all the same; doctors say that there is no emotion which more readily ravishes our judgement from its proper seat. I myself have seen many men truly driven out of their minds by fear, and it is certain that, while the fit lasts, fear engenders even in the most staid of men a terrifying confusion.

I leave aside simple folk, for whom fear sometimes conjures up visions of their great-grandsires rising out of their graves still wrapped in their shrouds, or else of chimeras, werewolves or goblins; but even among soldiers, where fear ought to be able to find very little room, how many times have I seen it change a flock of sheep into a squadron of knights in armour; reeds or bulrushes into men-at-arms and lancers; our friends, into enemies; a white cross into a red one.

When Monsieur de Bourbon captured Rome, a standard-bearer who was on guard at the Burgo San

Pietro was seized by such terror at the first alarm that he leapt through a gap in the ruins and rushed out of the town straight for the enemy still holding his banner; he thought he was running into the town, but at the very last minute he just managed to see the troops of Monsieur de Bourbon drawing up their ranks ready to resist him (it was thought that the townsfolk were making a sortie); he realised what he was doing and headed back through the very same gap out of which he had just made a three-hundred-yards' dash into the battlefield.

But the standard-bearer of Captain Juille was not so lucky when Saint-Pol was taken from us by Count de Bures and the Seigneur de Reu; for fear had made him so distraught that he dashed out of the town, banner and all, through a gun-slit and was cut to pieces by the attacking soldiers. There was another memorable case during the same siege, when fear so strongly seized the heart of a certain nobleman, freezing it and strangling it, that he dropped down dead in the breach without even being wounded.

Such fear can sometimes take hold of a great crowd. In one of the engagements between Germanicus and the Allemani two large troops of soldiers took fright and fled opposite ways, one fleeing to the place which the other had just fled from.

Sometimes fear as in the first two examples puts wings on our heels; at others it hobbles us and nails our feet to the ground, as happened to the Emperor

Theophilus in the battle which he lost against the Agarenes; we read that he was so enraptured and so beside himself with fear, that he could not even make up his mind to run away: '*adeo pavor etiam auxilia formidat*' [so much does fear dread even help]. Eventually Manuel, one of the foremost commanders of his army, shook him and pulled him roughly about as though rousing him from a profound sleep, saying, 'If you will not follow me I will kill you; the loss of your life matters less than the loss of the Empire if you are taken prisoner.'

Fear reveals her greatest power when she drives us to perform in her own service those very deeds of valour of which she robbed our duty and our honour. In the first pitched battle which the Romans lost to Hannibal during the consulship of Sempronius, an army of ten thousand foot-soldiers took fright, but seeing no other way to make their cowardly escape they fought their way through the thick of the enemy, driving right through them with incredible energy, slaughtering a large number of Carthaginians but paying the same price for a shameful flight as they should have done for a glorious victory.

It is fear that I am most afraid of. In harshness it surpasses all other mischances. What emotion could ever be more powerful or more appropriate than that felt by the friends of Pompey who were aboard a ship with him and witnessed that horrible massacre of his forces? Yet even that emotion was stifled by their fear of the Egyptian sails as they began to draw nearer; it was noticed that his friends had no time for anything but urging the sailors to strive to save them by rowing harder; but after they touched land at Tyre their fear left them and they were free to turn their thoughts to the losses they had just suffered and to give rein to those tears and lamentations which that stronger emotion of fear had kept in abeyance.

> *Tum pavor sapientiam omnem mihi ex animo expectorat.*
> [Then fear banishes all wisdom from my heart.]

Men who have suffered a good mauling in a military engagement, all wounded and bloody as they are, can be brought back to the attack the following day; but men who have tasted real fear cannot be brought even to look at the enemy again. People with a pressing fear of losing their property or of being driven into exile or enslaved also lose all desire to eat, drink or sleep, whereas those who are actually impoverished, banished or enslaved often enjoy life as much as anyone else. And many people, unable to withstand the stabbing pains of fear, have hanged themselves, drowned themselves or jumped to their deaths, showing us that fear is even more importunate and unbearable than death.

The Greeks acknowledged another species of fear over and above that fear caused when our reason is distraught; it comes, they say, from some celestial impulsion, without any apparent cause. Whole peoples have been seized by it as well as whole armies. Just such a fear brought wondrous desolation to Carthage: nothing was heard but shouts and terrified voices; people were seen dashing out of their houses as if the alarm had been sounded; they began attacking, wounding and killing each other, as though they took each other for enemies come to occupy their city. All was disorder and tumult until they had calmed the anger of their gods with prayer and sacrifice.

Such outbursts are called 'Panic terrors'.

– On the Power of the Imagination –

'*Fortis imaginatio generat casum*,' [A powerful imagination generates the event,] as the scholars say. I am one of those by whom the powerful blows of the imagination are felt most strongly. Everyone is hit by it, but some are bowled over. It cuts a deep impression into me: my skill consists in avoiding it not resisting it. I would rather live among people who are healthy and cheerful: the sight of another man's suffering produces physical suffering in me, and my own sensitivity has often misappropriated the feelings of a third party. A persistent cougher tickles my lungs and my throat.

The sick whom I am duty-bound to visit I visit more unwillingly than those with whom I feel less concerned and less involved. When I contemplate an illness I seize upon it and lodge it within myself: I do not find it strange that imagination should bring fevers and death to those who let it act freely and who give it encouragement.

In his own time Simon Thomas was a great doctor. I remember that I happened to meet him one day at the home of a rich old consumptive; he told his patient when discussing ways to cure him that one means was to provide occasions for me to enjoy his company: he

could then fix his eyes on the freshness of my countenance and his thoughts on the overflowing cheerful-
ness and vigour of my young manhood; by filling all his
senses with the flower of my youth his condition might
improve. He forgot to add that mine might get worse.

Gallus Vibius so tensed his soul to understand the
essence and impulsions of insanity that he toppled his
own judgement from its seat and was never able to restore it again: he could boast that he was made a fool
by his own wisdom.

Some there are who forestall the hand of their
executioners; one man was on the scaffold, being un-
blindfolded so that his pardon could be read to him,
when he fell down dead, the blow being struck by his
imagination alone. When imaginary thoughts trouble
us we break into sweats, start trembling, grow pale or
flush crimson; we lie struck supine on our feather-beds
and feel our bodies agitated by such emotions; some
even die from them. And boiling youth grows so hot in
its armour-plate that it consummates its sexual desires
while fast asleep in a dream –

> *Ut quasi transactis sæpe omnibus rebus profundant*
> *Fluminis ingentes fluctus, vestemque cruentent.*
> [So that, as though they had actually completed the act, they
> pour forth floods of semen and pollute their garments.]

It is no new thing for a man to wake up with cuckold's
horns which he never had when he went to bed, but

it is worth remembering what happened to Cyppus, a king in Italy: he had been very excited by a bullfight one day and his dreams that night had filled his head full of bulls' horns: thereupon horns grew on his forehead by the sheer power of his imagination.

Nature had denied the power of speech to the son of Croesus: passion gave it to him; Antiochus fell into a fever from the beauty of Stratonice, which was too vigorously imprinted on his soul; Pliny says that, on the very day of the wedding, he saw Lucius Cossitius change from woman to man; Pontanus and others tell of similar metamorphoses which have happened in Italy in recent centuries. And, since both Iphis' own desires and her mother's were so vehement,

> *Vota puer solvit, quae foemina voverat Iphis.*
> [Iphis fulfilled as a boy vows made as a girl.]

I was travelling though Vitry-le-François when I was able to see a man to whom the Bishop of Soissons had given the name of Germain at his confirmation: until the age of twenty-two he had been known by sight to all the townsfolk as a girl called Marie. He was then an old man with a full beard; he remained unmarried. He said that he had been straining to jump when his male organs suddenly appeared. (The girls there still have a song in which they warn each other not to take great strides lest they become boys, 'like Marie Germain'.) It is not surprising that this sort of occurrence happens frequently. For if the imagination does have any power in such matters, in girls it dwells so constantly and so forcefully on sex that it can (in order to avoid the necessity of so frequently recurring to the same thoughts and harsh yearnings) more easily make that male organ into a part of their bodies.

The scars of King Dagobert and of Saint Francis are attributed by some to the power of their imagination: and they say that by it bodies are sometimes transported from their places; Celsus gives an account of a priest whose soul was enraptured in such an ecstasy that for a considerable period his body remained breathless and senseless. Saint Augustine gives the name of another priest who only needed to hear lamentations and plaintive cries to fall into a swoon, being carried so vigorously outside himself that, until he came back to life again, in vain would you shake him about, shout at him, pinch him or sear his flesh: the priest said he heard their voices, but as though coming from afar; he was also aware of the bruising and branding. That this was no stubborn concealing of his sense-impressions is shown by his being, during this time, without pulse or breath.

It is likely that the credit given to miracles, visions, enchantments and such extraordinary events chiefly derives from the power of the imagination acting mainly on the more impressionable souls of the common people. Their capacity to believe has been so powerfully ravished that they think they see what they do not see. I am moreover of the opinion that those ridiculous attacks of magic impotence by which our society believes itself to be so beset that we talk of nothing else can readily be thought of as resulting from the impress of fear or apprehension. I know this from the experience of a man whom I can vouch for as though he were myself: there is not the slightest suspicion of sexual inadequacy in his case nor of magic spells; but he heard one of his comrades tell how an extraordinary impotency fell upon him just when he could least afford it; then, on a similar occasion, the horror of this account struck his own imagination so brutally that he too incurred a similar fate; from then on he was subject to relapses, the ignoble memory of his misadventure taunting him and tyrannising over him. He found that this madness he could cure by another kind of madness: he admitted beforehand that he was subject to this infirmity and spoke openly about it, so relieving the tensions within his soul; by bearing the malady as something to be expected, his sense of constriction grew less and weighed less heavily upon him; then (his thoughts being unencumbered and relaxed) when an occasion arose to its liking, his body, finding itself in good trim for first sounding itself out, seizing itself and taking itself by surprise with its partner in the know, clean cured itself of that condition. Except for genuine impotence, never again are you incapable if you are capable of doing it once.

This misfortune is to be feared only in adventures

where our souls are immoderately tense with desire and respect; especially when the opportunity is pressing and unforeseen, there is no means of recovering from this confusion. I know one man who found it useful to bring to it a body on the point of being satisfied elsewhere, in order to quieten the ardour of this frenzy and who, growing older, finds himself less impotent for being less potent.

Yet another found it helpful when a friend assured him that he was furnished with a counter-battery of enchantments certain to preserve him. I had better tell how that happened.

A highly placed Count with whom I was intimate was marrying a most beautiful lady who had long been courted by a guest present at the festivities; those who loved him were worried about him – especially one of his relations, an old lady who was presiding over the marriage (which was being held in her house): she feared there might be sorcery about and told me of it. I begged her to put her trust in me. I happened to have in my strong-boxes a certain little flat piece of gold on which were engraved celestial symbols, protecting against sunstroke and relieving headaches when correctly applied to the cranial suture; it was sewn on to a ribbon to be tied under the chin to keep it in place – a piece of lunacy akin to the one we are talking of. This peculiar present had been given me by Jacques Peletier: I decided to get some good out of it. I told the Count that he might well incur the same misfortune as

others and that there were those who would willingly
see that he did so: but he should go to the marriage-
bed confidently since I would do him a friendly turn,
not failing in his moment of need to perform a miracle
which lay within my power, provided that he promised
me on his honour to keep it most faithfully secret, simply giving me a sign if things had gone badly when we
rushed in with the festive supper. Both his soul and his
ears had received such a battering that, because of his
troubled imagination, he had indeed been incapable of
an erection: so he gave me the sign. He was then to get
up (I had told him) under pretence of chasing us out,
playfully seize the night-shirt I was holding (we were
much the same size) and wear it until he had followed
my prescription – which was as follows: as soon as we
had left the room he was to withdraw to pass water: he
was then to say certain prayers three times and make
certain gestures: each time he was to tie round himself
the ribbon I had put into his hand and carefully lay the
attached medallion over his kidneys, with the figure in
a specified position. Having done so, he should draw
the ribbon tight so that it could not come undone: then
he was to go back and confidently get on with the job,
not forgetting to throw my night-shirt over his bed in
such a way as to cover them both.

It is such monkeyings-about which mainly produce results: our thoughts cannot free themselves from
the convictions that such strange actions must derive
from some secret lore. Their weight and respect come

from their inanity. In short the figures on my talisman proved to have more to do with Venus than with the Sun, more potent in action than as a prophylactic.

I was led to do this deed (which is so foreign to my nature) by a rash and troubled humour. I am opposed to all feigned and subtle actions; I hate sleight of hand not only in games but even when it serves a purpose. The way is vicious even if the deed is not.

Amasis, a King of Egypt, wed Laodice, a very beautiful Grecian maiden. He was a pleasant companion in every other way, but he was incapable of lying with her; he threatened to kill her, thinking there had been some witchcraft. Appropriately enough where mental apprehensions are concerned, she deflected his attention towards invocations: having made his vows and prayers to Venus, he found that very night, after his sacrificial oblations, that he had been divinely restored.

Women are wrong to greet us with those affected provocative appearances of unwillingness which snuff out our ardour just as they kindle it. The daughter-in-law of Pythagoras used to say that a woman who lies with a man should doff her modesty with her kirtle and don it again with her shift. The heart of an attacker is easily dismayed when disturbed by calls to arms which are many and diverse; it is a bad start, once imagination makes a man suffer this shame (which she only does in those first encounters, since they are tempestuous and eager: it is in the first encounter that one most fears a defeat); this occurrence then puts him into a feverish moodiness which persists when subsequent opportunities arise.

Married folk have time at their disposal: if they are not ready they should not try to rush things. Rather than fall into perpetual wretchedness by being struck with despair at a first rejection, it is better to fail to make it properly on the marriage-couch, full as it is of feverish agitation, and to wait for an opportune moment, more private and less challenging. Before possessing his wife, a man who suffers a rejection should make gentle assays and overtures with various little sallies; he should not stubbornly persist in proving himself inadequate once and for all. Those who know that their member is naturally obedient should merely take care to out-trick their mental apprehensions.

We are right to note the licence and disobedience of this member which thrusts itself forward so inopportunely when we do not want it to, and which so inopportunely lets us down when we most need it; it imperiously contests for authority with our will: it stubbornly and proudly refuses all our incitements, both mental and manual. Yet if this member were arraigned for rebelliousness, found guilty because of it and then retained me to plead its cause, I would doubtless cast suspicion on our other members for having deliberately brought a trumped-up charge, plotting to arm everybody against it and maliciously accusing it alone of a defect common to them all. I ask you to reflect whether there is one single part of our body which does not often refuse to function when we want it to, yet does so when we want it not to. Our members have emotions proper to themselves which arouse them or quieten them down without leave from us. How often do compelling facial movements bear witness to thoughts which we were keeping secret, so betraying us to those who are with us? The same causes which animate that member animate – without our knowledge – the heart, the lungs and the pulse: the sight of some pleasant object can imperceptibly spread right through us the flame of a feverish desire. Is it only the veins and muscles of that particular member which rise or fall without the consent of our will or even of our very thoughts? We do not command our hair to stand on end with fear nor our flesh to quiver with desire. Our hands often go where we do not tell them; our tongues can fail, our voices congeal, when *they* want to. Even when we have nothing for the pot and would fain order our hunger and thirst not to do so, they never fail to stir up those members which are subject to them, just as that other appetite does: it also deserts us, inopportunely, whenever it wants to. That sphincter which serves to discharge our stomachs has dilations and contractions proper to itself, independent of our wishes or even opposed to them; so do those members which are destined to discharge the kidneys.

To show the limitless authority of our wills, Saint Augustine cites the example of a man who could make his behind produce farts whenever he would: Vives in his glosses goes one better with a contemporary example of a man who could arrange to fart in tune with verses recited to him; but that does not prove the pure obedience of that member, since it is normally most indiscreet and disorderly. In addition I know one Behind so stormy and churlish that it has obliged its master to fart forth wind constantly and unremittingly for forty years and is thus bringing him to his death.

Yet against our very will (on behalf of whose rights we have drawn up this bill of accusation) can be brought a prima-facie charge of sedition and rebellion because of its own unruliness and disobedience. Does it always wish what we want it to? Does it not often wish what we forbid it to – and that to our evident prejudice? Is it any more subject to the determinations of our reason? Finally, on behalf of my noble client, may it please the Court to consider that, in this matter, my client's case is indissolubly conjoined to a consort from whom he cannot be separated. Yet the suit is addressed to my client alone, employing arguments and making charges which (granted the properties of the Parties) can in no wise be brought against the aforesaid consort. By which it can be seen the manifest animosity and legal impropriety of the accusers. The contrary notwithstanding, Nature registers a protest against the barristers' accusations and the judges' sentences, and will meanwhile proceed as usual, as one who acted rightly when she endowed the aforesaid member with its own peculiar privilege to be the author of the only immortal achievement known to mortals. For which reason, generation is held by Socrates to be god-like, and Love, that desire for immortality, to be himself. *Daemon* and immortal.

One man, perhaps by the power of his imagination, leaves in France the very scrofula which his fellow then takes back into Spain. That is why it is customary to insist in such matters that the soul lend her consent. Why do doctors first work on the confidence of their patient with so many fake promises of a cure if not to allow the action of the imagination to make up for the trickery of their potions? They know that one of the masters of their craft told them in writing that there are men for whom it is enough merely to look at a medicine for it to prove effective.

That sudden whim of mine all came back to me because of a tale told me by one of my late father's servants who was an apothecary. He was a simple man – a Swiss (a people little given to vanity and lying). He had had a long acquaintance with a sickly merchant in Toulouse who suffered from the stone; he had frequent need of enemas and made his doctors prescribe him various kinds, depending on the symptoms of his illness. When the enemas were brought in, none of the usual formalities were omitted: he often used to finger them to see if they were too hot. There he was, lying down and turned on his side; all the usual preliminaries were gone through . . . except that no clyster was injected! After this ceremony the apothecary withdrew; the patient was treated as though he had taken the clyster and the result was the same as for those who had. If the doctor found that the treatment did not prove effective he gave him two or three other enemas – all of the same kind! Now my informant swears that the sick man's wife (in order to cut down expenses, since he paid for these clysters as though he had really had them) assayed simply injecting warm water; that proved to have no effect: the trickery was therefore discovered but he was obliged to return to the first kind.

There was a woman who believed she had swallowed a pin in her bread; she yelled and screamed as though she felt an insufferable pain in her throat where she thought she could feel it stuck; but since there was no swelling nor external symptoms, one clever fellow concluded that it was all imagination and opinion occasioned by a crust that had jabbed her on the way down; he made her vomit and secretly tossed a bent pin into what she had brought up. That woman believed that she had vomited it out and immediately felt relieved of the pain.

I know of a squire who had entertained a goodly company in his hall and then, four or five days later, boasted as a joke (for there was no truth in it) that he had made them eat cat pie; one of the young ladies in the party was struck with such horror at this that she collapsed with a serious stomach disorder and a fever: it was impossible to save her.

Even the very beasts are subject to the power of the imagination just as we are. Witness dogs, which grieve to death when they lose their masters. We can also see dogs yapping and twitching in their dreams, while horses whinny and struggle about.

But all this can be attributed to the close stitching of mind to body, each communicating its fortunes to the other. It is quite a different matter that the imagination should sometimes act not merely upon its own body but on someone else's. One body can inflict an illness on a neighbouring one (as can be seen in the case of the plague, the pox and conjunctivitis which are passed on from person to person):

> *Dum spectant oculi læsos, læduntur et ipsi:*
> *Multaque corporibus transitione nocent.*
> [Looking at sore eyes can make your own eyes sore; and many ills are spread by bodily infection.]

Similarly when the imagination is vehemently shaken it sends forth darts which may strike an outside object. In antiquity it was held that when certain Scythian women were animated by anger against anybody they could kill him simply by looking at him. Tortoises and ostriches hatch out their eggs by sight alone – a sign that they emit certain occult influences. And as for witches, they are said to have eyes which can strike and harm:

Nescio quis teneros oculus mihi fascinat agnos
[An eye, I know not whose, has bewitched my tender
lambs.]

For me magicians provide poor authority. All the
same we know from experience that mothers can transmit to the bodies of children in their womb marks connected with their thoughts – witness that woman who
gave birth to a blackamoor. And near Pisa there was
presented to the Emperor Charles, King of Bohemia,
a girl all bristly and hairy whom her mother claimed to
have conceived like this because of a portrait of John
the Baptist hanging above her bed. It is the same with
animals: witness Jacob's sheep and those partridges
and hares which are turned white by the snow in the
mountains. In my own place recently a cat was seen
watching a bird perched high up a tree; they stared
fixedly at each other for some little time when the bird
tumbled dead between the paws of the cat: either its
own imagination had poisoned it or else it had been
drawn by the cat's force of attraction. Those who are
fond of hawking know the tale of the falconer who
fixed his gaze purposefully on a kite as it flew and bet
he could bring it down by the sheer power of his sight.
And he did.

Or so they say: for when I borrow *exempla* I commit them to the consciences of those I took them from.
The discursive reflexions are my own and depend on
rational proof not on experience: everyone can add his

own examples; if anyone has none of his own he should not stop believing that such *exempla* exist, given the number and variety of occurrences. If my *exempla* do not fit, supply your own for me. In the study I am making of our manners and motives, fabulous testimonies – provided they remain possible – can do service as well as true ones. Whether it happened or not, to Peter or John, in Rome or in Paris, it still remains within the compass of what human beings are capable of; it tells me something useful about that. I can see this and profit by it equally in semblance as in reality. There are often different versions of a story: I make use of the one which is rarest and most memorable. There are some authors whose aim is to relate what happened: mine (if I could manage it) would be to relate what can happen. When details are lacking Schoolmen are rightly permitted to posit probabilities. I do not: where this is concerned I excel all historical fidelity in my devoted scrupulousness. Whenever my *exempla* concern what I have heard, what I have said or what I have done, I have not dared to allow myself to change even the most useless or trivial of circumstances. I do not know about my science, but not one jot has been consciously falsified.

While on this topic I often wonder how Theologians or philosophers and their like, with their exquisite consciences and their exacting wisdom, can properly write history. How can they pledge their own trustworthiness on the trustworthiness of ordinary people? How can they vouch for the thoughts of people they have never known and offer their own conjectures as sound coinage? They would refuse to bear sworn witness in Court about complex actions which actually occurred in their presence; there is no man so intimate with them that they would undertake to give a full account of all his thoughts.

I think it less risky to write about the past than the present, since the author has only to account for borrowed truth. Some have invited me to write about contemporary events, reckoning that I see them with eyes less vitiated by passion than others do and that I have a closer view than they, since Fortune has given me access to the various leaders of the contending parties. What they do not say is that I would not inflict such pain upon myself for all the fame of Sallust (being as I am the sworn enemy of binding obligations, continuous toil and perseverance), nor that nothing is so foreign to my mode of writing than extended narration. I have to break off so often from shortness of wind that neither the structure of my works nor their development is worth anything at all; and I have a more-than-childish ignorance of the words and phrases used in the most ordinary affairs. That is why I have undertaken to talk about only what I know how to talk about, fitting the subject-matter to my capacities. Were I to choose a subject where I had to be led, my capacities might prove inadequate to it. They do not say either that, since my freedom is so very free, I could have published judgements which even I would reasonably and readily hold to be unlawful and deserving of punishment. Of his own achievement Plutarch would be the first to admit that if his *exempla* are wholly and entirely true that is the work of his sources: his own work consisted in making them useful to posterity, presenting them with a splendour which lightens our path towards virtue.

An ancient account is not like a doctor's prescription, every item in it being tother or which.

– On the Cannibals –

When King Pyrrhus crossed into Italy, after noting the excellent formation of the army which the Romans had sent ahead towards him he said, 'I do not know what kind of Barbarians these are' (for the Greeks called all foreigners Barbarians) 'but there is nothing barbarous about the ordering of the army which I can see!' The Greeks said the same about the army which Flaminius brought over to their country, as did Philip when he saw from a hill-top in his kingdom the order and plan of the Roman encampment under Publius Sulpicius Galba. We should be similarly wary of accepting common opinions; we should judge them by the ways of reason not by popular vote.

I have long had a man with me who stayed some ten or twelve years in that other world which was discovered in our century when Villegaignon made his landfall and named it *La France Antartique*. This discovery of a boundless territory seems to me worthy of reflection. I am by no means sure that some other land may not be discovered in the future, since so many persons, greater than we are, were wrong about this one! I fear that our eyes are bigger than our bellies, our curiosity more than we can stomach. We grasp at everything but clasp nothing but wind.

Plato brings in Solon to relate that he had learned from the priests of the town of Saïs in Egypt how, long ago before the Flood, there was a vast island called Atlantis right at the mouth of the Straits of Gibraltar, occupying an area greater than Asia and Africa combined; the kings of that country, who not only possessed that island but had spread on to the mainland across the breadth of Africa as far as Egypt and the length of Europe as far as Tuscany, planned to stride over into Asia and subdue all the peoples bordering on the Mediterranean as far as the Black Sea. To this end they had traversed Spain, Gaul and Italy and had reached as far as Greece when the Athenians withstood them; but soon afterwards those Athenians, as well as the people of Atlantis and their island, were engulfed in that Flood.

It is most likely that that vast inundation should have produced strange changes to the inhabitable areas of the world; it is maintained that it was then that the sea cut off Sicily from Italy –

> *Hæc loca, vi quondam et vasta convulsa ruina,*
> *Dissiluisse ferunt, cum protinus utraque tellus*
> *Una foret.*
> [Those places, they say, were once wrenched apart by a
> violent convulsion, whereas they had formerly been one
> single land.]

– as well as Cyprus from Syria, and the island of Negro-
pontus from the Boeotian mainland, while elsewhere
lands once separated were joined together by filling in
the trenches between them with mud and sand:

> *sterilisque diu palus aptaque remis*
> *Vicinas urbes alit, et grave sentit aratrum.*
> [Barren swamps which you could row a boat through
> now feed neighbouring cities and bear the heavy plough.]

Yet there is little likelihood of that island's being the
New World which we have recently discovered, for it
was virtually touching Spain; it would be unbelievable
for a flood to force it back more than twelve hundred
leagues to where it is now; besides our modern seamen
have already all but discovered that it is not an island
at all but a mainland, contiguous on one side with the
East Indies and on others with lands lying beneath
both the Poles – or that if it is separated from them, it
is by straits so narrow that it does not deserve the name
of 'island' on that account.

It seems that large bodies such as these are subject,
as are our own, to changes, some natural, some feverish. When I consider how my local river the Dordogne
has, during my own lifetime, been encroaching on
the right-hand bank going downstream and has taken
over so much land that it has robbed many buildings
of their foundation, I realise that it has been suffering
from some unusual upset: for if it had always gone on

like this or were to do so in the future, the whole face of the world would be distorted. But their moods change: sometimes they incline one way, then another: and sometimes they restrain themselves. I am not discussing those sudden floodings whose causes we know. By the coast-line in Médoc, my brother the Sieur d'Arsac can see lands of his lying buried under sand spewed up by the sea: the tops of some of the buildings are still visible: his rents and arable fields have been changed into very sparse grazing. The locals say that the sea has been thrusting so hard against them for some time now that they have lost four leagues of land. These sands are the sea's pioneer-corps: and we can see those huge shifting sand-dunes marching a half-league ahead in the vanguard, capturing territory.

The other testimony from Antiquity which some would make relevant to this discovery is in Aristotle – if that little book about unheard wonders is really his. He tells how some Carthaginians struck out across the Atlantic beyond the Straits of Gibraltar, sailed for a long time and finally discovered a large fertile island entirely clothed in woodlands and watered by great deep rivers but very far from any mainland; they and others after them, attracted by the richness and fertility of the soil, emigrated with their wives and children and started living there. The Carthaginian lords, seeing that their country was being gradually depopulated, expressly forbade any more to go there on pain of death and drove out those new settlers, fearing it is said that they would in time increase so greatly that they would supplant them and bring down their State.

But that account in Aristotle cannot apply to these new lands either.

That man of mine was a simple, rough fellow – qualities which make for a good witness: those clever chaps notice more things more carefully but are always adding glosses; they cannot help changing their story a little in order to make their views triumph and be more persuasive; they never show you anything purely as it is: they bend it and disguise it to fit in with their own views. To make their judgement more credible and to win you over they emphasise their own side, amplify it and extend it. So you need either a very trustworthy man or else a man so simple that he has nothing in him on which to build such false discoveries or make them plausible; and he must be wedded to no cause. Such was my man; moreover on various occasions he showed me several seamen and merchants whom he knew on that voyage. So I am content with what he told me, without inquiring what the cosmographers have to say about it.

What we need is topographers who would make detailed accounts of the places which they had actually been to. But because they have the advantage of visiting Palestine, they want to enjoy the right of telling us tales about all the rest of the world! I wish everyone would write only about what he knows – not in this matter only but in all others. A man may well have detailed knowledge or experience of the nature of one particular river or stream, yet about all the others he knows only what everyone else does; but in order to trot out his little scrap of knowledge he will write a book on the whole of physics! From this vice many great inconveniences arise.

Now to get back to the subject, I find (from what has been told me) that there is nothing savage or barbarous about those peoples, but that every man calls barbarous anything he is not accustomed to; it is indeed the case that we have no other criterion of truth or right-reason than the example and form of the opinions and customs of our own country. There we always find the perfect religion, the perfect polity, the most developed and perfect way of doing anything! Those 'savages' are only wild in the sense that we call fruits wild when they are produced by Nature in her ordinary course: whereas it is fruit which we have artificially perverted and misled from the common order which we ought to call savage. It is in the first kind that we find their true, vigorous, living, most natural and most useful properties and virtues, which we have bastardised in the other kind by merely adapting them to our corrupt tastes. Moreover, there is a delicious savour which even our taste finds excellent in a variety of fruits produced in those countries without cultivation: they rival our own. It is not sensible that artifice should be reverenced more than Nature, our great and powerful Mother. We have so overloaded the richness and beauty of her products by our own ingenuity that we have smothered her entirely. Yet wherever her pure light does shine, she wondrously shames our vain and frivolous enterprises:

> *Et veniunt ederæ sponte sua melius,*
> *Surgit et in solis formosior arbutus antris,*
> *Et volucres nulla dulcius arte canunt.*
> [Ivy grows best when left untended; the strawberry tree flourishes more beautifully in lonely grottoes, and birds sing the sweeter for their artlessness.]

All our strivings cannot even manage to reproduce the nest of the smallest little bird, with its beauty and appropriateness to its purpose; we cannot even reproduce the web of the wretched spider. Plato says that all things are produced by nature, fortune or art, the greatest and fairest by the first two, the lesser and least perfect by the last.

Those peoples, then, seem to me to be barbarous only in that they have been hardly fashioned by the mind of man, still remaining close neighbours to their original state of nature. They are still governed by the laws of Nature and are only very slightly bastardised by ours; but their purity is such that I am sometimes sometimes seized with irritation at their not having been discovered earlier, in times when there were men who could have appreciated them better than we do. It irritates me that neither Lycurgus nor Plato had any knowledge of them, for it seems to me that what experience has taught us about those peoples surpasses not only all the descriptions with which poetry has beautifully painted the Age of Gold and all its ingenious fictions about Man's blessed early state, but also the very conceptions and yearnings of philosophy. They could not even imagine a state of nature so simple and so pure as the one we have learned about from experience; they could not even believe that societies of men could be maintained with so little artifice, so little in the way of human solder. I would tell Plato that those people have no trade of any kind, no acquaintance with writing, no knowledge of numbers, no terms for governor or political superior, no practice of subordination or of riches or poverty, no contracts, no inheritances, no divided estates, no occupation but leisure, no concern for kinship – except such as is common to them all – no clothing, no agriculture, no metals, no use of wine or corn. Among them you hear no words for treachery, lying, cheating, avarice, envy, backbiting or forgiveness. How remote from such perfection would Plato find that Republic which he thought up – *'viri a diis recentes'* [men fresh from the gods].

> *Hos natura modos primum dedit.*
> [These are the ways which Nature first ordained.]

In addition they inhabit a land with a most delightful countryside and a temperate climate, so that, from what I have been told by my sources, it is rare to find anyone ill there; I have been assured that they never saw a single man bent with age, toothless, blear-eyed or tottering. They dwell along the sea-shore, shut in to landwards by great lofty mountains, on a stretch of land some hundred leagues in width. They have fish and flesh in abundance which bear no resemblance to ours; these they eat simply cooked. They were so horror-struck by the first man who brought a horse there and rode it that they killed him with their arrows before they could recognise him, even though he had had dealings with them on several previous voyages. Their dwellings are immensely long, big enough to hold two or three hundred souls; they are covered with the bark of tall trees which are fixed into the earth, leaning against each other in support at the top, like some of our barns where the cladding reaches down to the ground and acts as a side. They have a kind of wood so hard that they use it to cut with, making their swords from it as well as grills to cook their meat. Their beds are woven from cotton and slung from the roof like hammocks on our ships; each has his own, since wives sleep apart from their husbands. They get up at sunrise and have their meal for the day as soon as they do so; they have no other meal but that one. They drink nothing with it, like those Eastern peoples who, according to Suidas, only drink apart from meals. They drink together several times a day, and plenty of it. This drink is made from a certain root and has the colour of our claret. They always drink it lukewarm; it only keeps for two or three days; it tastes a bit sharp, is in no ways heady and is good for the stomach; for those who are not used to it it is laxative but for those who are, it is a very pleasant drink. Instead of bread they use a certain white product resembling coriander-cakes. I have tried some: it tastes sweet and somewhat insipid.

They spend the whole day dancing; the younger men go off hunting with bow and arrow. Meanwhile some of the women-folk are occupied in warming up their drink: that is their main task. In the morning, before their meal, one of their elders walks from one end of the building to the other, addressing the whole barnful of them by repeating one single phrase over and over again until he has made the rounds, their building being a good hundred yards long. He preaches two things only: bravery before their enemies and love for their wives. They never fail to stress this second duty, repeating that it is their wives who season their drink and keep it warm. In my own house, as in many other places, you can see the style of their beds and ropework as well as their wooden swords and the wooden bracelets with which they arm their wrists in battle, and the big open-ended canes to the sound of which they maintain the rhythm of their dances. They shave off all their hair, cutting it more cleanly than we do, yet with razors made of only wood or stone. They believe in the immortality of the soul: souls which deserve well of the gods dwell in the sky where the sun rises; souls which are accursed dwell where it sets. They have some priests and prophets or other, but they rarely appear among the people since they live in the mountains. When they do appear they hold a great festival and a solemn meeting of several villages – each of the barns which I have described constituting a village situated about one French league distant from the next. The prophet then addresses them in public, exhorting them to be virtuous and dutiful, but their entire system of ethics contains only the same two articles: resoluteness in battle and love for their wives. He foretells what is to happen and the results they must expect from what they undertake; he either incites them to war or deflects them from it, but only on condition that if he fails to divine correctly and if things turn out other than he foretold, then – if they can catch him – he is condemned as a false prophet and hacked to pieces. So the prophet who gets it wrong once is seen no more.

Prophecy is a gift of God. That is why abusing it should be treated as a punishable deceit. Among the Scythians, whenever their soothsayers got it wrong they were shackled hand and foot and laid in ox-carts full of bracken where they were burned. Those who treat subjects under the guidance of human limitations can be excused if they have done their best; but those who come and cheat us with assurances of powers beyond the natural order and then fail to do what they promise, should they not be punished for it and for the foolhardiness of their deceit?

These peoples have their wars against others further inland beyond their mountains; they go forth
naked, with no other arms but their bows and their
wooden swords sharpened to a point like the blades of
our pig-stickers. Their steadfastness in battle is astonishing and always ends in killing and bloodshed: they
do not even know the meaning of fear or flight. Each
man brings back the head of the enemy he has slain
and sets it as a trophy over the door of his dwelling. For
a long period they treat captives well and provide them
with all the comforts which they can devise; afterwards
the master of each captive summons a great assembly
of his acquaintances; he ties a rope to one of the arms
of his prisoner and holds him by it, standing a few feet
away for fear of being caught in the blows, and allows
his dearest friend to hold the prisoner the same way by
the other arm: then, before the whole assembly, they
both hack at him with their swords and kill him. This
done, they roast him and make a common meal of him,
sending chunks of his flesh to absent friends. This is
not as some think done for food – as the Scythians used
to do in antiquity – but to symbolise ultimate revenge.
As a proof of this, when they noted that the Portuguese
who were allied to their enemies practised a different
kind of execution on them when taken prisoner –
which was to bury them up to the waist, to shoot show-
ers of arrows at their exposed parts and then to hang
them – they thought that these men from the Other
World, who had scattered a knowledge of many a vice

41

throughout their neighbourhood and who were greater masters than they were of every kind of revenge, which must be more severe than their own; so they began to abandon their ancient method and adopted that one. It does not sadden me that we should note the horrible barbarity in a practice such as theirs: what does sadden me is that, while judging correctly of their wrong-doings we should be so blind to our own. I think there is more barbarity in eating a man alive than in eating him dead; more barbarity in lacerating by rack and torture a body still fully able to feel things, in roasting him little by little and having him bruised and bitten by pigs and dogs (as we have not only read about but seen in recent memory, not among enemies in antiquity but among our fellow-citizens and neighbours – and, what is worse, in the name of duty and religion) than in roasting him and eating him after his death.

Chrysippus and Zeno, the leaders of the Stoic school, certainly thought that there was nothing wrong in using our carcasses for whatever purpose we needed, even for food – as our own forebears did when, beleaguered by Caesar in the town of Alesia, they decided to relieve the hunger of the besieged with the flesh of old men, women and others who were no use in battle:

> *Vascones, fama est, alimentis talibus usi*
> *Produxere animas.*
> [By the eating of such food it is notorious that the
> Gascons prolonged their lives.]

And our medical men do not flinch from using corpses in many ways, both internally and externally, to cure us. Yet no opinion has ever been so unruly as to justify treachery, disloyalty, tyranny and cruelty, which are everyday vices in us. So we can indeed call those folk barbarians by the rules of reason but not in comparison with ourselves, who surpass them in every kind of barbarism. Their warfare is entirely noble and magnanimous; it has as much justification and beauty as that human malady allows: among them it has no other foundation than a zealous concern for courage. They are not striving to conquer new lands, since without toil or travail they still enjoy that bounteous Nature who furnishes them abundantly with all they need, so that they have no concern to push back their frontiers. They are still in that blessed state of desiring nothing beyond what is ordained by their natural necessities: for them anything further is merely superfluous. The generic term which they use for men of the same age is 'brother'; younger men they call 'sons'. As for the old men, they are the 'fathers' of everyone else; they bequeath all their goods, indivisibly, to all these heirs in common, there being no other entitlement than that with which Nature purely and simply endows all her creatures by bringing them into this world. If the neighbouring peoples come over the mountains to attack them and happen to defeat them, the victors' booty consists in fame and in the privilege of mastery in virtue and valour: they have no other interest in the

43

goods of the vanquished and so return home to their own land, which lacks no necessity; nor do they lack that great accomplishment of knowing how to enjoy their mode-of-being in happiness and to be content with it. These people do the same in their turn: they require no other ransom from their prisoners-of-war than that they should admit and acknowledge their defeat – yet there is not one prisoner in a hundred years who does not prefer to die rather than to derogate from the greatness of an invincible mind by look or by word; you cannot find one who does not prefer to be killed and eaten than merely to ask to be spared. In order to make their prisoners love life more they treat them generously in every way, but occupy their thoughts with the menaces of the death awaiting all of them, of the tortures they will have to undergo and of the preparations being made for it, of limbs to be lopped off and of the feast they will provide. All that has only one purpose: to wrench some weak or unworthy word from their lips or to make them wish to escape, so as to enjoy the privilege of having frightened them and forced their constancy.

Indeed, if you take it the right way, true victory consists in that alone:

> *victoria nulla est*
> *Quam quæ confessos animo quoque subjugat hostes.*
> [There is no victory unless you subjugate the minds of the enemy and make them admit defeat.]

In former times those warlike fighters the Hungarians never pressed their advantage beyond making their enemy throw himself on their mercy. Once having wrenched this admission from him, they let him go without injury or ransom, except at most for an undertaking never again to bear arms against them.

Quite enough of the advantages we do gain over our enemies are mainly borrowed ones not truly our own. To have stronger arms and legs is the property of a porter not of Valour; agility is a dead and physical quality, for it is chance which causes your opponent to stumble and which makes the sun dazzle him; to be good at fencing is a matter of skill and knowledge which may light on a coward or a worthless individual. A man's worth and reputation lie in the mind and in the will: his true honour is found there. Bravery does not consist in firm arms and legs but in firm minds and souls: it is not a matter of what our horse or our weapons are worth but of what we are. The man who is struck down but whose mind remains steadfast, '*si succiderit, de genu pugnat*' [if his legs give way, then on his knees doth he fight]; the man who relaxes none of his mental assurance when threatened with imminent death and who faces his enemy with inflexible scorn as he gives up the ghost is beaten by Fortune not by us: he is slain but not vanquished. Sometimes it is the bravest who may prove most unlucky. So there are triumphant defeats rivalling victories; Salamis, Plataea, Mycale and Sicily are the fairest sister-victories which the Sun has ever seen, yet they would never dare to compare their combined glory with the glorious defeat of King Leonidas and his men at the defile of Thermopylae. Who has ever run into battle with a greater desire and ambition for victory than did Captain Ischolas when he was defeated? Has any man ever assured his safety more cleverly or carefully than he assured his destruction? His task was to defend against the Arcadians a certain pass in the Peleponnesus. He realised that he could not achieve this because of the nature of the site and of the odds against him, concluding that every man who faced the enemy must of necessity die in the battlefield; on the other hand he judged it unworthy of his own courage, of his greatness of soul and of the name of Sparta to fail in his duty; so he chose the middle path between these two extremes and acted thus: he saved the youngest and fittest soldiers of his unit to serve for the defence of their country and sent them back there. He then determined to defend that pass with men whose loss would matter less and who would, by their death, make the enemy purchase their breakthrough as dearly as possible. And so it turned out. After butchering the Arcadians who beset them on every side, they were all put to the sword. Was ever a trophy raised to a victor which was not better due to those who were vanquished? True victory lies in your role in the conflict, not in coming through safely: it consists in the honour of battling bravely not battling through.

To return to my tale, those prisoners, far from

yielding despite all that was done to them during the two or three months of their captivity, maintain on the contrary a joyful countenance: they urge their captors to hurry up and put them to the test; they defy them, insult them and reproach them for cowardice and for all the battles they have lost against their country. I have a song made by one such prisoner which contains the following: Let them all dare to come and gather to feast on him, for with him they will feast on their own fathers and ancestors who have served as food and sustenance for his body. 'These sinews,' he said, 'this flesh and these veins – poor fools that you are – are your very own; you do not realise that they still contain the very substance of the limbs of your forebears: savour them well, for you will find that they taste of your very own flesh!' There is nothing 'barbarous' in the contriving of that topic. Those who tell how they die and who describe the act of execution show the prisoners spitting at their killers and pulling faces at them. Indeed, until their latest breath, they never stop braving them and defying them with word and look. It is no lie to say that these men are indeed savages – by our standards; for either they must be or we must be: there is an amazing gulf between their souls and ours.

The husbands have several wives: the higher their reputation for valour the more of them they have. One beautiful characteristic of their marriages is worth noting: just as our wives are zealous in thwarting our love and tenderness for other women, theirs are equally zealous in obtaining them for them. Being more concerned for their husband's reputation than for anything else, they take care and trouble to have as many fellow-wives as possible, since that is a testimony to their husband's valour.

– Our wives will scream that that is a marvel, but it is not: it is a virtue proper to matrimony, but at an earlier stage. In the Bible Leah, Rachel, Sarah and the wives of Jacob all made their fair handmaidens available to their husbands; Livia, to her own detriment, connived at the lusts of Augustus, and Stratonice the consort of King Deiotarus not only provided her husband with a very beautiful chambermaid who served her but carefully brought up their children and lent a hand in enabling them to succeed to her husband's rank.

– Lest anyone should think that they do all this out of a simple slavish subjection to convention or because of the impact of the authority of their ancient customs without any reasoning or judgement on their part, having minds so dulled that they could never decide to do anything else, I should cite a few examples of what they are capable of.

Apart from that war-song which I have just given an account of, I have another of their songs, a love-song, which begins like this:

> O Adder, stay: stay O Adder! From your colours
> let my sister take the pattern for a girdle
> she will make for me to offer to my love;

So may your beauty and your speckled hues be for
  ever honoured above all other snakes.

This opening couplet serves as the song's refrain. Now
I know enough about poetry to make the following
judgement: not only is there nothing 'barbarous' in
this conceit but it is thoroughly anacreontic. Their language incidentally is a pleasant one with an agreeable
sound and has terminations rather like Greek.

  Three such natives, unaware of what price in peace
and happiness they would have to pay to buy a knowledge of our corruptions, and unaware that such commerce would lead to their downfall – which I suspect to
be already far advanced – pitifully allowing themselves
to be cheated by their desire for novelty and leaving the
gentleness of their regions to come and see ours, were
at Rouen at the same time as King Charles IX. The
King had a long interview with them: they were shown
our manners, our ceremonial and the layout of a fair
city. Then someone asked them what they thought of
all this and wanted to know what they had been most
amazed by. They made three points; I am very annoyed
with myself for forgetting the third, but I still remember two of them. In the first place they said (probably
referring to the Swiss Guard) that they found it very
odd that all those full-grown bearded men, strong and
bearing arms in the King's entourage, should consent
to obey a boy rather than choosing one of themselves
as a Commander; secondly – since they have an idiom

in their language which calls all men 'halves' of one another – that they had noticed that there were among us men fully bloated with all sorts of comforts while their halves were begging at their doors, emaciated with poverty and hunger: they found it odd that those destitute halves should put up with such injustice and did not take the others by the throat or set fire to their houses.

I had a very long talk with one of them (but I used a stupid interpreter who was so bad at grasping my meaning and at understanding my ideas that I got little joy from it). When I asked the man (who was a commander among them, our sailors calling him a king) what advantage he got from his high rank, he told me that it was to lead his troops into battle; asked how many men followed him, he pointed to an open space to signify as many as it would hold – about four or five thousand men; questioned whether his authority lapsed when the war was over, he replied that he retained the privilege of having paths cut for him through the thickets in their forests, so that he could easily walk through them when he visited villages under his sway.

Not at all bad, that. – Ah! But they wear no breeches . . .

– On the Custom of Wearing Clothing –

Whichever way I want to go I find myself obliged to break through some barrier of custom, so thoroughly has she blocked all our approaches. During this chilly season I was chatting about whether the habit of those newly discovered peoples of going about stark naked was forced on them by the hot climate, as we say of the Indians and the Moors, or whether it is the original state of mankind. Since the word of God says that 'everything under the sun' is subject to the same law, in considerations such as these, where a distinction has to be made between natural laws and contrived ones, men of understanding regularly turn for advice to the general polity of the world: nothing can be counterfeit there. Now, since everything therein is exactly furnished with stitch and needle for maintaining its being, it is truly unbelievable that we men alone should have been brought forth in a deficient and necessitous state, a state which can only be sustained by borrowings from other creatures. I therefore hold that just as plants, trees, animals and all living things are naturally equipped with adequate protection from the rigour of the weather –

Proptereaque fere res omnes aut corio sunt,
Aut seta, aut conchis, aut callo, aut cortice tectæ
[Wherefore virtually everything is protected by hides,
silks, shells, tough skin or bark]

– so too were we; but like those who drown the light of
day with artificial light, we have drowned our natural
means with borrowed ones. It can easily be seen that
custom makes possible things impossible for us: for
some of the peoples who have no knowledge of clothing live under much the same climate as ourselves –
and even we leave uncovered the most delicate parts of
our bodies: our eyes, mouth, nose, ears and, in the case
of our peasants and forebears, the chest and the belly.
If we had been endowed at birth with undergarments
and trousers there can be no doubt that Nature would
have armed those parts of us which remained exposed
to the violence of the seasons with a thicker skin, as she
has done for our fingertips and the soles of our feet.

Why should this seem so hard to believe? The gulf
between the way I dress and the way my local peasant
does is wider than that between him and a man dressed
only in his skin. In Turkey especially many go about
naked for the sake of their religion.

In midwinter somebody or other asked one of our
local tramps who was wearing nothing but a shirt yet
remained as merry as a man swaddled up to his ears in
furs how he could stand it. 'You, Sir,' he replied, 'have
your face quite uncovered: myself am all face!'

The Italians tell a tale about (I think it was) the Duke of Florence's jester. He was poorly clad; his master asked him how he managed to stand the cold, which he himself found very troublesome. 'Do as I do,' he said, 'and you won't feel the cold either. Pile on every stitch you've got!'

Even when very old, King Massinissa could not be persuaded to wear anything on his head, come cold, wind or rain. And the same is told about the Emperor Severus.

Herodotus says that both he and others noted that, of those who were left dead in the battles between the Egyptians and the Persians, the Egyptians had by far the harder cranium: that was because the Persians always kept their heads covered first with boys' caps and then with turbans, whereas the Egyptians went close-cropped and bareheaded from childhood.

And King Agesilaus wore the same clothes, summer and winter, until he was decrepit. According to Suetonius, Caesar always led his armies, normally bare-headed and on foot, in sunshine as in rain. The same is said of Hannibal:

> *tum vertice nudo*
> *Excipere insanos imbres cælique ruinam.*
> [Bare-headed he withstood the furious rainstorms and the cloudbursts.]

A Venetian just back from the Kingdom of Pegu

where he had spent a long time writes that the men and women there cover all the rest of their body, but always go barefoot even on their horses. And Plato enthusiastically advises that, for the health of our entire body, we should give no other covering to head or foot than what Nature has put there.

The man whom the Poles elected King after our own monarch (and he is truly one of the greatest of princes) never wears gloves and never fails to wear the same hat indoors, no matter what the winter weather.

Whereas I cannot bear to go about with my buttons undone or my jacket unlaced, the farm-labourers in my neighbourhood would feel shackled if they did not do so. Varro maintains that when mankind was bidden to remain uncovered in the presence of gods and governors it was for our health's sake and to help us to endure the fury of the seasons rather than out of reverence.

While on the subject of cold, since the French are used to a medley of colours – not me though: I usually wear black and white like my father – let me switch subject and add that Captain Martin Du Bellay relates how he saw it freeze so hard during the Luxembourg expedition that the wine-ration had to be hacked at with axes, weighed out to the soldiers and carried away in baskets. Ovid is but a finger's breadth from that:

> *Nudaque consistunt formam servantia testæ*
> *Vina, nec hausta meri, sed data frusta bibunt.*

[The naked wine stands straight upright, retaining the shape of the jar: they do not swallow draughts of wine but chunks of it.]

It freezes so hard in the swampy distributaries of Lake Maeotis that in the very same spot where Mithridates' lieutenant fought dry-shod against his enemies and defeated them, he defeated them again, when summer came, in a naval engagement.

In their battle against the Carthaginians near Placentia, the Romans were at a great disadvantage since they had to charge while their blood was nipped and their limbs stiff with the cold, whereas Hannibal had caused fires to be lit throughout his camp to warm his soldiers and had also distributed an embrocation oil to his troops to rub in, thaw out their muscles and limber up, while clogging their pores against the penetrating blasts of the prevailing bitter wind.

The Greeks' homeward retreat from Babylon is famous for the hardships and sufferings they had to overcome. One was their encountering a dreadful snowstorm in the Armenian mountains; they lost all their bearings in that country and its roads; they were so suddenly beset that, with most of their mule-train dead, they went one whole day and night without food or drink; many of them met their deaths or were blinded by the hailstones and the glare of the snow; many had frostbitten limbs and many others remained conscious but were frozen stiff and unable to move.

Alexander came across a people where they bury their fruit trees in winter to protect them from the frost.

While on the subject of clothing, the King of Mexico changed four times a day and never wore the same clothes twice; his cast-off garments were constantly used for gifts and rewards; similarly no pot, plate, kitchen-ware or table-ware was ever served him twice.

– On Smells –

O f some such as Alexander the Great it is said that their sweat smelt nice (because of some rare complexion outside the natural Order, the cause of which was sought by Plutarch and others). But the normal fashioning of our bodies works contrary to that: the best characteristic we can hope for is to smell of nothing. The sweetness of the purest breath consists in nothing more excellent than to be without any offensive smell, as the breath of healthy children. That is why Plautus says, '*Mulier tum bene olet, ubi nihil olet*', 'A woman smells nice when she smells of nothing,' just as we say that the best perfume for her actions is for her to be quiet and discreet. And when people give off nice odours which are not their own we may rightly suspect them, and conclude that they use them to smother some natural stench. That is what gives rise to those adages of the ancient poets which claim that the man who smells nice in fact stinks:

> *Rides nos Coracine, nil olentes.*
> *Malo quam bene olere, nil olere.*
> [You laugh at us, Coracinus, because we emit no smell:
> I would rather smell of nothing than smell sweetly.]

And again,

> *Posthume, non bene olet, qui bene semper olet.*
> [A man who always smells nice, Posthumus, actually stinks.]

However I am myself very fond of living amongst good smells and I immeasurably loathe bad ones, which I sense at a greater distance than anyone else:

> *Namque sagacius units odoror,*
> *Polypus, an gravis hirsutis cubet hircus in alis,*
> *Quant canis acer ubi lateat sus.*
> [I have a nose with with more flair, Polypus, for sensing the goaty smell of hairy armpits than any hound on the track of a stinking hoar.]

The simpler, more natural smells seem to me to be the most agreeable. A concern for smells is chiefly a matter for the ladies. In deepest Barbary the Scythian women powder themselves after washing and smother their whole face and body with a certain sweet-smelling unguent, native to their soil; when they take off this cosmetic they find themselves smooth and nice-smelling for an approach to their menfolk.

Whatever the smell, it is wonderful how it clings to me and how my skin is simply made to drink it in. The person who complained that Nature left Man with no means of bringing smells to his nose was in error: smells do it by themselves. But, in my particular case the job is done for me by my thick moustache: if I bring my glove or my handkerchief anywhere near it, the smell will linger there all day. It gives away where I have just come from. Those close smacking kisses of my youth, gluey and greedy, would stick to it and remain there for hours afterwards. Yet I find myself little subject to those mass illnesses which are caught by social intercourse and spring from infected air; and I have been spared those of my own time, of which there have been several kinds in our towns and among our troops. We read that although Socrates never left Athens during several recurrences of the plague which so often racked that city, he alone suffered no harm.

It seems to me that doctors could make better use of smells than they do, for I have frequently noticed that, depending on which they are, they variously affect me and work upon my animal spirits; which convinces me of the truth of what is said about the invention of odours and incense in our Churches (a practice so ancient and so widespread among all nations and religions): that it was aimed at making us rejoice, exciting us and purifying us so as to render us more capable of contemplation.

In order to judge it I wish I had been invited to experience the culinary art of those chefs who know how to season wafting odours with the savour of various foods, as was particularly remarked in our time in the case of the King of Tunis who landed at Naples for face to face talks with the Emperor Charles. His meats were stuffed with sweet-smelling ingredients, so luxuriously that a peacock and two pheasants cost a hundred ducats to prepare in their manner. And when those birds were cut up they filled not merely the hall but all the rooms of his palace and even the neighbouring houses with a delicious mist which was slow to evaporate.

When choosing where to stay, my principal concern is to avoid air which is oppressive and stinking. My liking for those fair cities Venice and Paris is affected by the pungent smell of the marshes of one and the mud of the other.

– On the Length of Life –

I cannot accept the way we determine the span of our lives. I note that wise men shorten it considerably compared to the common opinion. 'What!' said Cato the Younger to those who wanted to stop him killing himself: 'Am I still at the age when you can accuse me of leaving life too soon?' Yet he was only forty-eight. He reckoned, considering how few men reach it, that his age was fully mature and well advanced. And those who keep themselves going with the thought that some span of life or other which they call 'natural' promises them a few years more could only do so provided that there was some ordinance exempting them personally from those innumerable accidents (which each one of us comes up against and is subject to by nature) which can rupture the course of life which they promise themselves.

What madness it is to expect to die of that failing of our powers brought on by extreme old age and to make that the target for our life to reach when it is the least usual, the rarest kind of death. We call that death, alone, a natural death, as if it were unnatural to find a man breaking his neck in a fall, engulfed, engulfed in a shipwreck, surprised by plague or pleurisy, and as though our normal condition did not expose us to all of those harms. Let us not beguile ourselves with such fine words: perhaps we ought, rather, to call natural anything which is generic, common to all and universal. Dying of old age is a rare death, unique and out of the normal order and therefore less natural than the others. It is the last, the uttermost way of dying; the farther it is from us, the less we can hope to reach it; it is indeed the limit beyond which we shall not go and which has been prescribed by Nature's law as never to be crossed: but it is a very rare individual law of hers which makes us last out till then. It is an exemption which she grants as an individual favour to one man in the space of two or three centuries, freeing him from the burden of those obstacles and difficulties which she strews along the course of that long progress.

Therefore my opinion is that we should consider whatever age we have reached as an age reached by few. Since in the normal course of events men never reach that far, it is a sign of that we are getting on. And since we have crossed the accustomed limits – and that constitutes the real measure of our days – we ought not to hope to get much farther beyond them; having escaped those many occasions of death which have tripped up all the others, we ought to admit that an abnormal fortune such as that which has brought us so far is indeed beyond the usual procedure and cannot last much longer.

It is a defect in our very laws to hold that false idea, for they do not admit that a man be capable of managing his affairs before the age of twenty-five, yet he can scarcely manage to make his life last that long! Augustus lopped five years off the old Roman ordinances and decreed that it sufficed to be thirty for a man to assume the office of judge. Servius Tullius exempted knights who had passed the age of forty-seven from obligatory war-service; Augustus remitted it at forty-five. Sending men into inactivity before fifty-five or sixty does not seem very right to me. I would counsel extending our vocations and employments as far as we could in the public interest; the error is on the other side, I find: that of not putting us to work soon enough. The man who had power to decide everything in the whole world at nineteen wanted a man to be thirty before he could decide where to place a gutter!

Personally I reckon that our souls are free from their bonds at the age of twenty, as they ought to be, and that by then they show promise of all they are capable of. No soul having failed by then to give a quite evident pledge of her power ever gave proof of it afterwards. By then – or never at all – natural qualities and capacities reveal whatever beauty or vigour they possess.

> *Si l'espine nou pique quand nai,*
> *A peine que piqu jamai*
> [If a thorn pricks not at its birth,
> It will hardly prick at all]

as they say in Dauphiné.

Of all the fair deeds of men in ancient times and in our own which have come to my knowledge, of whatever kind they may be, I think it would take me longer to enumerate those which were made manifest before the age of thirty than after. Yes, and often in the lives of the very same men: may I not say that with total certainty in the case of Hannibal and his great adversary Scipio? They lived a good half of their lives on the glory achieved in their youth: they were great men later compared with others, but not great compared with themselves. As for me, I am convinced that, since that age, my mind and my body have not grown but diminished, and have retreated not advanced.

It may well be that (for those who make good use of their time) knowledge and experience grow with the years but vitality, quickness, firmness and other qualities which are more truly our own, and more important, more ours by their essence, droop and fade.

> *Ubi jam validis quassatum est viribus ævi*
> *Corpus, et obtusis ceciderunt viribus artus,*
> *Claudicat ingenium, delirat linguaque mensque.*
> [When the body is shattered by the mighty blows of age and our limbs shed their blunted powers, our wits too become lame and our tongues and our minds start to wander.]

Sometimes it is the body which is the first to surrender to old age, sometimes too the soul; and I have known plenty of men whose brains grew weak before their stomachs or their legs; and it is all the more dangerous an infirmity in that the sufferer is hardly aware of it and its symptoms are not clear ones.

But now I am complaining not that the laws allow us to work so late but that they are so late in putting us to work.

It seems to me that, considering the frailty of our life and the number of natural hazards to which it is exposed, we should not allow so large a place in it to being born, to leisure and to our apprenticeship.

– On the Inconstancy of Our Actions –

T hose who strive to account for a man's deeds are never more bewildered than when they try to knit them into one whole and to show them under one light, since they commonly contradict each other in so odd a fashion that it seems impossible that they should all come out of the same shop. Young Marius now acts like a son of Mars, now as a son of Venus. They say that Pope Boniface VIII took up his duties like a fox, bore them like a lion and died like a dog. And who would ever believe that it was Nero, the very image of cruelty, who when they presented him with the death-sentence of a convicted criminal to be duly signed replied, 'Would to God that I had never learned to write!' so much it oppressed his heart to condemn a man to death?

Everything is so full of such examples (indeed each man can furnish so many from himself) that I find it strange to find men of understanding sometimes taking such trouble to match up the pieces, seeing that vacillation seems to me to be the most common and blatant defect of our nature: witness the famous line of Publius the author of farces:

Malum consilium est, quod mutari non potest!
[It's a bad resolution which can never be changed!]

It seems reasonable enough to base our judgement of a man on the more usual features of his life: but given the natural inconstancy of our behaviour and our opinions it has often occurred to me that even sound authors are wrong in stubbornly trying to weave us into one invariable and solid fabric.

They select one universal character, then, following that model, they classify and interpret all the actions of a great man; if they cannot twist them the way they want they accuse the man of insincerity. Augustus did get away from them: for there is in that man throughout his life a diversity of actions so clear, so sudden and so uninterrupted that they had to let him go in one piece, with no verdict made on him by even the boldest judges. Of Man I can believe nothing less easily than invariability: nothing more easily than variability. Whoever would judge a man in his detail, piece by piece, separately, would hit on the truth more often.

It is difficult to pick out more than a dozen men in the whole of Antiquity who groomed their lives to follow an assured and definite course, though that is the principal aim of wisdom. To sum it all up and to embrace all the rules of Man's life in one word, 'Wisdom,' said an Ancient, 'is always to want the same thing, always *not* to want the same thing.' I would not condescend to add, he said, 'provided that your willing be right. For if it is not right, it is impossible for it to remain ever one and the same.'

I was once taught indeed that vice is no more than a defect and irregularity of moderation, and that consequently it is impossible to tie it to constancy. There is a saying attributed to Demosthenes: the beginning of all virtue is reflection and deliberation: its end and perfection, constancy. If by reasoning we were to adopt one definite way, the way we chose would be most beautiful of all; but nobody has thought of doing that.

> *Quod petiit, spernit, repetit quod nuper omisit;*
> *Æstuat, et vitae disconvenit ordine toto.*
> [Judgement scorns what it yearned for, yearns again for what it recently spurned; it shifts like the tide and the whole of life is disordered.]

Our normal fashion is to follow the inclinations of our appetite, left and right, up and down, as the winds of occasion bear us along. What we want is only in our thought for the instant that we want it: we are like that creature which takes on the colour of wherever you put it. What we decided just now we will change very soon; and soon afterwards we come back to where we were: it is all motion and inconstancy:

> *Ducimur ut nervis alienis mobile lignum.*
> [We are led like a wooden puppet by wires pulled by others.]

We do not *go:* we are borne along like things afloat, now bobbing now lashing about as the waters are angry or serene.

> *Nonne videmus*
> *Quid sibi quisque velit nescire, et quærere semper,*
> *Commutare locum, quasi onus deponere possit?*
> [Surely we see that nobody knows what he wants, that he is always looking for something, always changing his place, as though he could cast off his burden?]

Every day a new idea: and our humours change with the changes of weather:

> *Tales sunt hominum mentes, quali pater ipse*
> *Juppiter auctifero lustravit lumine terras.*
> [The minds of men are such as Father Juppiter changes them to, as he purifies the world with his fruitful rays.]

We float about among diverse counsels: our willing of anything is never free, final or constant.

If a man were to prescribe settled laws for a settled government established over his own brain, then we would see, shining throughout his whole life, a calm uniformity of conduct and a faultless interrelationship between his principles and his actions.

– (The defect in the Agrigentines noted by Empedocles was their abandoning themselves to pleasure as though they were to die the next day, while they built as though they would never die at all.) –

It would be easy enough to explain the character of such a man; that can be seen from the younger Cato: strike one of his keys and you have struck them all; there is in him a harmony of sounds in perfect concord such as no one can deny. In our cases on the contrary every one of our actions requires to be judged on its own: the surest way in my opinion would be to refer each of them to its context, without looking farther and without drawing any firm inference from it.

During the present debauchery of our wretched commonwealth I was told about a young woman near where I then was who had thrown herself from a high window to avoid being forced by some beggarly soldier billeted on her. She was not killed by her fall and repeated her attempt by trying to slit her own throat with a knife; she was stopped from doing so, but only after she had given herself a nasty wound. She herself admitted that the soldier had not yet gone beyond importuning her with requests, solicitations and presents, but she was afraid that he would eventually use force. And above all this, there were the words she used, the look on her face and that blood testifying to her chastity, truly like some second Lucretia. Now I learned as a fact that both before and after this event she was quite wanton and not all that hard to get. It is like the moral in that tale: 'However handsome and noble you may be, when you fail to get your end in do not immediately conclude that your lady is inviolably chaste: it does not mean that the mule-driver is not having better luck with her.'

Antigonus had grown to love one of his soldiers for his virtue and valour and ordered his doctors to treat him for a malignant internal complaint which had long tormented him; he noticed that, once the soldier was cured, he set about his work with much less ardour and asked him who had changed him into such a coward. 'You yourself, Sire,' he replied, 'by freeing me from the weight of those pains which made me think life was worth nothing.'

Then there was the soldier of Lucullus who had been robbed of everything by the enemy and who, to get his own back, made a fine attack against them. After he had plucked enough enemy feathers to make up for his loss Lucullus, who had formed a high opinion of him, began urging some hazardous exploit upon him with all the fairest expostulations he could think of:

> *Verbis quae timido quoque possent addere mentem.*
> [With words enough to give heart to a coward.]

'You should try urging that,' he replied, 'on some wretched soldier who has lost everything' –

> *quantumvis rusticus ibit,*
> *Ibit eo, quo vis, qui zonam perdidit, inquit*
> [yokel though he was, he replied: 'The man who will go anywhere you like is the one who has just lost his money-belt']–

and he absolutely refused to go.

When we read that after Mechmet had insulted and berated Chasan the chief of his Janissaries for allowing his line of battle to be broken by the Hungarians and for fighting faint-heartedly, Chasan's only reply was, alone and just as he was, weapon in hand, to charge madly against the first group of enemy soldiers to come along, who promptly overwhelmed him: that may well have been not so much an act of justification as a change of heart; not so much natural bravery as a new feeling of distress.

That man you saw yesterday so ready to take risks: do not think it odd if you find him craven tomorrow. What had put heart into his belly was anger, or need, or his fellows, or wine, or the sound of a trumpet. His heart had not been fashioned by reasoned argument: it was those factors which stiffened it; no wonder then if he has been made quite different by other and contrary factors.

The changes and contradictions seen in us are so flexible that some have imagined that we have two souls, others two angels who bear us company and trouble us each in his own way, one turning us towards good the other towards evil, since such sudden changes cannot be accommodated to one single entity.

Not only does the wind of chance events shake me about as it lists, but I also shake and disturb myself by the instability of my stance: anyone who turns his prime attention on to himself will hardly ever find himself in the same state twice. I give my soul this face or that, depending upon which side I lay it down on. I speak about myself in diverse ways: that is because I look at myself in diverse ways. Every sort of contradiction can be found in me, depending upon some twist or attribute: timid, insolent; chaste, lecherous; talkative, taciturn; tough, sickly; clever, dull; brooding, affable; lying, truthful; learned, ignorant; generous, miserly and then prodigal – I can see something of all that in myself, depending on how I gyrate; and anyone who studies himself attentively finds in himself and in his very judgement this whirring about and this discordancy. There is nothing I can say about myself as a whole simply and completely, without intermingling and admixture. The most universal article of my own Logic is DISTINGUO.

I always mean to speak well of what is good, and to interpret favourably anything that can possibly be taken that way; nevertheless, so strange is our human condition that it leads to our being brought by vice itself to 'do good', except that 'doing good' is to be judged solely by our intentions. That is why one courageous action must not be taken as proof that a man really is brave; a man who is truly brave will always be brave on all occasions. If a man's valour were habitual and not a sudden outburst it would make him equally resolute in all eventualities: as much alone as with his comrades, as much in a tilt-yard as on the battlefield; for, despite what they say, there is not one valour for the town and another for the country. He would bear with equal courage an illness in his bed and a wound in battle, and would no more fear dying at home than in an attack. We would never see one and the same man charging into the breach with brave assurance and then raging like a woman over the loss of a lawsuit or a son. If he cannot bear slander but is resolute in poverty; if he cannot bear a barber-surgeon's lancet but is unyielding against the swords of his adversaries, then it is not the man who deserves praise but the deed. Cicero says that many Greeks cannot even look at an enemy yet in sickness show constancy: the Cimbrians and the Celtiberians on the contrary; '*nihil enim potest esse æquabile, quod non a certa ratione proficiscatur.*' [For nothing can be called constant which does not arise out of a fixed principle.]

There is no valour greater in its kind than Alexander's; yet it is but one kind of valour; it is not in all cases sufficiently whole or all-pervasive. Absolutely incomparable it may be, but it has its blemishes, with the result that we see him worried to distraction over the slightest suspicion he may have that his men are plotting against his life, and see him conducting his investigations with an injustice so chaotic and ecstatic and with a fear which overturned his natural reason. Then there is the superstition from which he so markedly suffered: it bears some image of faint-heartedness. And the excessive repentance he showed for murdering Clytus is another testimony to the inconstancy of his mind.

We are fashioned out of oddments put together – '*voluptatem contemnunt, in dolore sunt molliores; gloriam negligunt, franguntur infamia*' [they despise pleasure but are rather weak in pain; they are indifferent to glory, but are broken by disgrace] – and we wish to win honour under false flags. Virtue wants to be pursued for her own sake: if we borrow her mask for some other purpose then she quickly rips it off our faces. Virtue, once the soul is steeped in her, is a strong and living dye which never runs without taking the material with her.

That is why to judge a man we must follow his tracks long and carefully. If his constancy does not rest firmly upon its own foundations; '*cui vivendi via considerata atque provisa est*'; [the path which his life follows having been thought about and prepared for beforehand;] if various changes make him change his pace – I mean his *path*, for his pace may be hastened by them or made heavy and slow – then let him go free, for that man will always 'run with the wind', *A vau le vent*, as the crest of our Lord Talbot puts it.

No wonder, said an Ancient, that chance has so much power over us, since it is by chance that we live. Anyone who has not groomed his life in general towards some definite end cannot possibly arrange his individual actions properly. It is impossible to put the pieces together if you do not have in your head the idea of the whole. What is the use of providing yourself with paints if you do not know what to paint? No man

sketches out a definite plan for his life; we only determine bits of it. The bowman must first know what he
is aiming at: then he has to prepare hand, bow, bow-
string, arrow and his drill to that end. Our projects go
astray because they are not addressed to a target. No
wind is right for a seaman who has no predetermined
harbour. I do not agree with the verdict given in favour of Sophocles in the action brought against him
by his son, which argued, on the strength of seeing a
performance of one of his tragedies, that he was fully
capable of managing his domestic affairs. Neither do I
agree that the inferences drawn by the Parians sent to
reform the Milesian government justified the conclu-
sion they reached: visiting the island they looked out
for the best-tended lands and the best-run country
estates and, having noted down their owners' names,
summoned all the citizens of the town to assemble
and appointed those owners as the new governors
and magistrates, judging that those who took care of
their private affairs would do the same for the affairs
of state.

We are entirely made up of bits and pieces, woven together so diversely and so shapelessly that each
one of them pulls its own way at every moment. And
there is as much difference between us and ourselves
as there is between us and other people. '*Magnam rem
puta unum hominem agere*' [Let me convince you that it
is a hard task to be always the same man.] Since ambition can teach men valour, temperance and generosity

– and, indeed, justice; since covetousness can plant in the mind of a shop-boy, brought up in obscurity and idleness, enough confidence to cast himself on the mercy of the waves and angry Neptune in a frail boat, far from his hearth and home, and also teach him discernment and prudence; and since Venus herself furnishes resolution and hardiness to young men still subject to correction and the cane, and puts a soldier's heart into girls still on their mothers' knees:

> *Hac duce, custodes furtim transgressa jacentes,*
> *Ad Juvenem tenebris sola puella venit:*
> [With Venus as her guide, the maiden, quite alone,
> comes to the young man, sneaking carefully through her
> sleeping guardians:]

it is not the act of a settled judgement to judge us simply by our outward deeds: we must probe right down inside and find out what principles make things move; but since this is a deep and chancy undertaking, I would that fewer people would concern themselves with it.

– On Drunkenness –

T he world is all variation and dissimilarity. Vices are all the same in that they are vices – and doubtless the Stoics understand matters after that fashion: but even though they are equally vices they are not equal vices. That a man who has overstepped by a hundred yards those limits

> *quos ultra citraque nequit consistere rectum,*
> [beyond which, and short of which, there is no right way,]

should not be in a worse condition than a man who has only overstepped them by ten yards is not believable; nor that sacrilege should be no worse than stealing a cabbage from our garden:

> *Nec vincet ratio, tantumdem ut peccet idemque*
> *Qui teneros caules alieni fregerit horti,*
> *Et qui nocturnus divum sacra legerit.*
> [Reason cannot convince me that there is equal sinfulness in trampling down someone's spring cabbages and in robbing the temple-treasures in the night.]

There is as much diversity in vice as in anything else.

It is dangerous to confound the rank and importance of sins: murderers, traitors and tyrants gain too much by it. It is not reasonable that they should be able to salve their consciences because somebody else is lazy, lascivious or not assiduous in his prayers. Each man comes down heavily on his neighbours' sins and lessens the weight of his own. Even the doctors of the Church often rank sins badly to my taste.

Just as Socrates said that the prime duty of wisdom is to distinguish good from evil, we, whose best always partakes of vice, should say the same about knowing how to distinguish between the vices: if that is not done exactingly, the virtuous man and the vicious man will be jumbled unrecognisedly together.

Now drunkenness, considered among other vices, has always seemed to me gross and brutish. In others our minds play a larger part; and there are some vices which have something or other magnanimous about them, if that is the right word. There are some which are intermingled with learning, diligence, valour, prudence, skill and *finesse*: drunkenness is all body and earthy. Moreover the grossest nation of our day is alone in honouring it. Other vices harm our intellect: this one overthrows it; and it stuns the body:

> *cum vini vis penetravit,*
> *Consequitur gravitas membrorum, præpediuntur*
> *Crura vacillanti, tardescit lingua, madet mens,*
> *Nant oculi; clamor, singultus, jurgia gliscunt.*

79

[when the strength of the wine has sunk in, our limbs become heavy, we stagger and trip over our legs; our speech becomes slow; our mind, sodden; our eyes are a-swim. Then comes the din, the hiccoughs and the fights.]

The worst state for a man is when he loses all consciousness and control of himself.

And among other things they say that, just as the must fermenting in the wine-jar stirs up all the lees at the bottom, so too does wine unbung the most intimate secrets of those who have drunk beyond measure:

> *tu sapientium*
> *Curas et arcanum jocoso*
> *Consilium retegis Lyæo.*
> [in those jolly Bacchic revels you, my wine-jar, uncover worries and the secret counsels of the wise.]

Josephus tells how he wheedled secrets out of an ambassador sent to him by his enemies by making him drink a lot. Nevertheless Augustus confided his most private secrets to Lucius Piso, the conqueror of Thrace, and was never let down; nor was Tiberius let down by Cossus on whom he unburdened all of his plans: yet we know that those two men were so given to drinking that they had often to be carried out of the Senate, both drunk,

> *Externo inflatum venas de more Lyæo.*
> [With veins swollen with others' wine, as usual.]

And the plan to kill Caesar was well kept when confided to Cassius, who drank water, but also when confided to Cimber, who often got drunk; which explains his joking reply: 'Should I bear the weight of a tyrant, when I cannot bear the weight of my wine!' Even our German mercenaries when drowned in their wine remember where they are quartered, the password and their rank:

> *nec facilis victoria de madidis, et*
> *Blæsis, atque mero titubantibus.*
> [it is not easy to beat them, even when they are sodden-drunk, incoherent and staggering about.]

I would never have thought anybody could be buried so insensibly in drunkenness if I had not read the following in the history books. With the purpose of inflicting on him some notable indignity, Attalus invited to supper that Pausanias who, on this very subject, later killed Philip King of Macedonia (a king whose fine qualities nevertheless bore witness to the education he had received in the household and company of Epaminondas). He got him to drink so much that he could bring him, quite unaware of what he was doing, to abandon his fair body to mule-drivers and to many of the most abject scullions in his establishment, as if it were the body of some whore in a hedgerow.

And then there is the case told me by a lady whom I honour and hold in the greatest esteem: towards

Castres, near Bordeaux, where her house is, there was a village woman, a widow of chaste reputation, who, becoming aware of the first hints that she might be pregnant, told the women of the neighbourhood that if only she had a husband she would think she was expecting. But as the reason for her suspicions grew bigger every day and finally became evident, she was reduced to having a declaration made from the pulpit in her parish church, stating that if any man would admit what he had done she promised to forgive him and, if he so wished, to marry him. One of her young farm-labourers took courage at this proclamation and stated that he had found her one feast-day by her fireside after she had drunk her wine freely; she was so deeply and provocatively asleep that he had been able to have her without waking her up. They married each other and are still alive.

Antiquity, certainly, did not greatly condemn this vice. The very writings of several philosophers speak of it indulgently; even among the Stoics there are those who advise you to let yourself drink as much as you like occasionally and to get drunk so as to relax your soul:

> *Hoc quoque virtutum quondam certamine, magnum*
> *Socratem palmam promeruisse ferunt.*
> [They say that Socrates often carried off the prize in this trial of strength too.]

That Censor and corrector of others, Cato was re-proached for his heavy drinking:

> *Narratur et prisci Catonis*
> *Sæpe mero caluisse virtus.*
> [It is told how the virtue of old Cato was often warmed with wine].

Such a famous King as Cyrus cited among the praiseworthy qualities which made him preferable to his brother Artaxerxes the fact that he knew how to drink better. Even among the best regulated and best governed peoples it was very common to assay men by making them drunk. I have heard one of the best doctors in Paris, Silvius, state that it is a good thing once a month to arouse our stomachs by this excess so as to stop their powers from getting sluggish and to stimulate them in order to prevent their growing dull. And we can read that the Persians discussed their most important affairs after drinking wine.

My taste and my complexion are more hostile than my reason to this vice. For, leaving aside the fact that I readily allow my beliefs to be captive to the Ancients, I find this vice base and stultifying but less wicked and a cause of less harm than the others, which virtually all do more direct public damage to our society. And if, as they maintain, we can never enjoy ourselves with-out it costing us something, I find that this vice costs our conscience less than the others: besides it is not a negligible consideration that it is easy to provide for and easy to find.

A man advanced in years and rank told me that he counted drink among the three main pleasures left to him in this life. But he set about it in the wrong way; for fine palates and an anxious selecting of wine are to be absolutely avoided. If you base your pleasure on drinking good wine you are bound to suffer from sometimes drinking bad. Your taste ought to be more lowly and more free. To be a good drinker you must not have too tender a palate. The Germans enjoy drinking virtually any wine. Their aim is to gulp it rather than to taste it. They get a better bargain. Their pleasure is more abundant and closer at hand.

Secondly, to drink in the French style at both meals, but moderately for fear of your health, is too great a restraint on the indulgence of god Bacchus: more time and constancy are required. The Ancients spent entire nights in this occupation and often went on into the next day. So we should train our habit in wider firmer ways. I have seen in my time a great lord, a person famous for his successes in several expeditions of high importance, who effortlessly and in the course of his ordinary meals never drank less than two gallons of wine and who, after that, never showed himself other than most sage and well-advised in the conduct of our affairs.

We should allow more time to that pleasure which we wish to count on over the whole of our lives. Like shop-apprentices and workmen we ought to refuse no opportunity for a drink; we ought always to have the desire for one in our heads: it seems that we are cutting down this particular one all the time and that, as I saw as a boy, dinner parties, suppers, and late-night feasts used to be much more frequent and common in our houses than they are now. Could we really be moving towards an improvement in something at least! Certainly not. It is because we throw ourselves into lechery much more than our fathers did. Those two occupations impede each other's strength. On the one hand lechery has weakened our stomachs: on the other, sober drinking has rendered us vigorous and lively in our love-making.

It is wonderful what accounts I heard my father give of the chastity of his times. He had the right to say so, as he was both by art and nature most graceful in the company of ladies. He talked little and well; he intermingled his speech with elegant references to books in the vernacular, especially Spanish, and among the Spanish he frequently cited the so-called *Marco Aurelio*. His face bore an expression of gentle seriousness, humble and very modest; he took particular care to be respectable and decent in his person and his dress both on horse and on foot. He was enormously faithful to his word and, in all things, conscientious and meticulous, tending rather towards over-scrupulousness. For a small man he was very strong, straight and well-proportioned; his face was pleasing and rather brown;

he was skilled and punctilious in all gentlemanly sports. I have also seen some canes filled with lead with which he is said to have exercised his arms for throwing the bar and the stone or for fencing, as well as shoes shod with lead to improve his running and jumping. Folk recall little miracles of his at the long-jump. When he was over sixty I remember him laughing at our own agility by vaulting into the saddle in his furry gown, by putting his weight on his thumb and leaping over a table and by never going up to his room without jumping three or four steps at a time. But more to my subject, he said that there was hardly one woman of quality in the whole province who was ill-spoken of, and he would tell of men – especially himself – who were on remarkably intimate terms with decent women without a breath of suspicion. In his own case he solemnly swore that he came virgin to his marriage-bed; and yet he had long done his bit in the transalpine wars, leaving a detailed diary of events there, both public and personal. And he married on his return from Italy in 1528 at the mature age of thirty-three.

Let us get back to our bottles.

The disadvantages of old age (which has need of support and renewal) could reasonably give birth to a desire for drink, since a capacity for wine is virtually the last pleasure which the passing years steal from us.

According to our drinking fraternity natural heat first gets a hold on our feet; that concerns our childhood; from there it rises to our loins where it long settles in, producing there if you ask me the only true bodily pleasures of this life: in comparison, the other pleasures are half asleep. Finally, like a mist rising and evaporating, it lands in the gullet and makes there its last abode.

For all that, I do not understand how anyone can prolong the pleasure of drinking beyond his thirst, forging in his mind an artificial appetite which is contrary to nature. My stomach would never get that far: it has enough bother dealing with what it takes in for its needs. I am so constituted that I care little for drink except at dessert; that is why my last draught is usually my biggest. Anacharsis was amazed that the Greeks should drink out of bigger glasses at the end of their meals; it was I think for the same reason that the Germans do: that is when they start their drinking contests.

Plato forbids young people to drink before the age of eighteen and to get drunk before forty. But men over forty he tells to enjoy it and to bring copiously into their banquets the influence of Dionysius, that kind god who restores gaiety to grown men and youth to the old ones, who calms and softens the passions of the soul just as iron is softened by the fire. And in his *Laws* he considers convivial drinking to be useful (provided that the group has a leader to ensure that order is maintained), since getting drunk is a good and certain trial of each man's character and, at the same time, has the property of giving older men the idea of enjoying themselves in music and dancing, useful pastimes which they would not dare to engage in when of settled mind. Wine also has the capacity of tempering the soul and giving health to the body. Nevertheless he liked the following restrictions, partly borrowed from the Carthaginians: that it should be done without on military expeditions; that all statesmen and judges should abstain when about to perform their duties and to deliberate on matters of public concern; that the daytime should be avoided – that is owed to other activities – as well as any night when we intend to beget children.

They say that the philosopher Stilpo, weighed down by old age, deliberately hastened his death by drinking his wine without water. A similar cause suffocated the failing powers of the aged philosopher Arcesilaus, but that was unintentional.

Whether the soul of a wise man should be such as to surrender to the power of wine is an old and entertaining question:

> Si 'munitae adhibet vim sapientiae'.
> [Whether 'wine should be able to make an assault on secure wisdom'.]

To what inanities are we driven by that good opinion we men have of ourselves! The best governed Soul in the world has quite enough to do to stay on her feet and to keep herself from falling to the ground from her own weakness. Not one in a thousand can stand up calm and straight for one instant in her life; it can even be doubted, given her natural condition, whether she ever can. But if you add constancy as well, then that is her highest perfection: I mean if nothing should shake it, something which hundreds of events can do. It was no good that great poet Lucretius philosophising and bracing himself: a love-potion drove him insane. Do they think that an apoplexy will not make Socrates lose his wits as much as a porter? Some have forgotten their own names by the force of an illness, and a light wound has struck down the judgement of others. A man can be as wise as he likes: he is still a man; and what is there more frail, more wretched, more a thing of nothing, than man? Wisdom cannot force our natural properties:

> *Sudores itaque et pallorem existere toto*
> *Corpore, et infringi linguam, vocemque aboriri,*
> *Caligare oculos, sonere aures, succidere artus,*
> *Denique concidere ex animi terrore videmus.*
> [Then we see sweat and pallor take over his whole body, his tongue grows incoherent, his voice fails, his eyes are troubled, his ears begin to ring, his legs give way and he falls to the ground, as panic seizes his mind.]

When he is threatened with a blow nothing can stop a man closing his eyes, or trembling if you set him on the edge of a precipice, just like a child, Nature reserving to herself these signs of her authority, signs slight but unattackable by reason or Stoic virtue, in order to teach Man that he is mortal and silly. He becomes livid with fear; he reddens with shame; he bewails an attack of colic paroxysms if not with a loud cry of despair at least with a cry which is broken and wheezing.

> *Humani a se nihil alienum putet!*
> [Let him realise that nothing human is a stranger to him!]

Poets who can make up anything they like dare not relieve their heroes even of the burden of weeping:

> *Sic fatur lachrymans, classique immittit habenas.*
> [Thus spoke Aeneas through his tears and his fleet sailed unbridled away.]

It suffices that a man should rein in his affections and moderate them, for it is not in his power to suppress them. And my very own Plutarch – so perfect, so outstanding a judge of human actions – when confronted by Brutus and Torquatus killing their children was led to doubt whether virtue could really get that far, and whether those great men had not in fact been shaken by some passion or other. All actions which exceed the usual limits are open to sinister interpretations, since higher things are no more to our taste than inferior ones.

Let us leave aside that other School which makes an express profession of pride. Yet even in that third School which is reckoned to be the most indulgent of them all we hear similar boastings from Metrodorus: '*Occupavi te, Fortuna, atque cepi; omnesque aditus tuos interclusi, ut ad me aspirare non posses.*' [I have forestalled you, O Fortune and I have caught you; I have blocked off all your approaches, you cannot get near me.]

When Anaxarchus, on the orders of Nicocreon, Tyrant of Cyprus, was put into a stone mortar and beaten to death with blows from an iron pestle, he never ceased to cry, 'Go on! Strike, bash on, you are not pounding Anaxarchus but his casing'; when we hear our Christian martyrs shouting out to the tyrant from the midst of the flames, 'It is well roasted on this side; chop it off and eat it; it is cooked just right: now start on the other side'; when we hear in Josephus of the boy who was torn to pieces with clawed pincers and bored through by the bradawls of Antiochus, yet who still defied him, crying out in a firm assured voice: 'Tyrant! You are wasting your time! I am still here, quite comfortable! Where is this pain, where are those tortures you were threatening me with? Is this all you can do? My constancy hurts you more than your cruelty hurts me! You cowardly beggar! It is you who are surrendering: I am growing stronger! Make me lament, make me give way, make me surrender, if you can! Goad on your henchmen and your hangmen: they have lost heart and can do nothing more! Give them weapons! Egg them on!' – then we have to admit that there is some change for the worse in their souls, some frenzy, no matter how holy.

When we hear such Stoic paradoxes as, 'I would rather be raging mad than a voluptuary' – that is the saying of Antisthenes, – when Sextius tells us that he would rather be transfixed by pain than by pleasure; when Epicurus decides to treat gout as though it were tickling him, refuses rest and good health, light-heartedly defies ills and, despising less biting pains, will not condescend to struggle in combat against them but summons and even wishes for pains which are strong and anguishing and worthy of him:

> *Spumantemque dari pecora inter inertia votis*
> *Optat aprum, aut fulvum descendere monte leonem;*
> [Amidst his placid flock he prays to be vouchsafed some
> slavering boar, or that some wild lion will come down
> from the mountain;]

who does not conclude that those are the cries of a mind which is leaping out of its lodgings? Our Soul cannot reach so high while remaining in her own place. She has to leave it and rise upwards and, taking the bit between her teeth, bear her man off, enrapture him away so far that afterwards he is amazed by what he has done; just as in war, the heat of the combat often makes the valiant soldiers take such hazardous steps that they are the first to be struck with astonishment once they have come back to themselves; so too the poets are often seized by amazement by their own works and no longer recognise the defiles through which they had passed at so fine a gallop. In their case too it is called frenzy and mania. And just as Plato says that a sedate man knocks in vain at poetry's door, so too Aristotle says that no outstanding soul is free from a mixture of folly. He is right to call *folly* any leap – however praiseworthy it might be – which goes beyond our reason and our discourse. All the more so in that wisdom is a controlled handling of our soul, carried out, on our Soul's responsibility, with measure and proportion.

Plato contends that the faculty of prophesying is 'above ourselves'; that we must be 'outside ourselves' when we accomplish it; our prudence must be darkened by some sleep or illness, or else snatched out of its place by a heavenly rapture.

– On Cowardice,
the Mother of Cruelty –

I have often heard it said that cowardice is the moth-er of cruelty. And I have learned from experience that that harsh rage of wicked inhuman minds is usual-ly accompanied by womanish weakness. I have known the cruellest of men to cry easily for the most frivolous of causes. The Tyrant Alexander of Pheres could not bear to hear tragedies performed in the amphitheatre for fear that the citizens might see him, who had with-out pity put many to death every day, blubbering over the misfortunes of Hecuba and Andromache. Can it be a weakness in their soul which makes such men sus-ceptible to every extreme? Valour (which acts only to overcome resistance) –

Nec nisi bellantis gaudet cervice juvenci
[And which takes no delight in killing even a bull unless unless it resists] –

stops short when it sees the enemy at its mercy. But pu-sillanimity, so as to join in the festivities even though it could not have any role in the first act, chooses its role in the second: that of blood and slaughter. Murders after victory are normally done by the common people and the men in charge of the baggage-train; and what makes us, witness so many unheard of cruelties in these people's wars of ours is that the common riff-raff become used to war and swagger about, up to their arms in blood, hacking at a body lying at their feet since they can conceive of no other valour:

> *Et lupus et turpes instant morientibus ursi,*
> *Et quæcunque minor nobilitate fera est,*
> [The wolves and base bears fall on the dying, and so do all the more ignoble beasts,]

like the cowardly curs which, in our homes, snap and tear at the skins of wild beasts which they would not dare to attack in the field.

What is it that makes all our quarrels end in death nowadays? Whereas our fathers knew degrees of vengeance we now begin at the end and straightway talk of nothing but killing. What causes that, if not cowardice? Everyone knows that there is more bravery in beating an enemy than in finishing him off; more contempt in making him bow his head than in making him die; that, moreover, the thirst for vengeance is better slaked and satisfied by doing so, since the only intention is to make it felt. That is why we do not attack a stone or an animal if it hurts us, since they are incapable of feeling our revenge. To kill a man is to shield him from our attack.

And just as Bias cried out to a wicked man, 'I

know you will be punished sooner or later, but I am afraid afraid I shall never live to see it'; and just as he sympathised with the Orchomenians because the chastisement of Lyciscus' treachery against them came at a time when there was nobody left who had suffered by it whom such chastisement would have gratified the most: vengeance is at its most wretched when it is wreaked upon someone who has lost the means of feeling it; for, as the one who seeks revenge wishes to see it if he is to enjoy it, the one who receives it must see it too if he is to suffer the pain and be taught a lesson.

'He'll be sorry for it,' we say. Do we really think he is sorry for it once we have shot him through the head? Quite the contrary: if we look closely we will find him cocking a snook as he falls: he does not even hold it against us. That is a long way from feeling sorry! And we do him one of the kindest offices of this life, which is to let him die quickly and painlessly. He is at rest while we have to scuttle off like rabbits, running away from the officers of the watch who are on our trail. Killing is all right for preventing some future offence but not for avenging one already done. It is a deed more of fear than of bravery; it is an act of caution rather than of courage; of defence rather than of attack. It is clear that by acting thus we give up both the true end of vengeance and all care for our reputation: we show we are afraid that if we let the man live he will do it again. By getting rid of him you act not against him but against yourself.

In the Kingdom of Narsinga their way of doing things would be no use to us. There, not only soldiers but even artisans settle their quarrels with their swords; their king never denies the field to any who would fight a duel, and, and in the case of men of quality he honours it with his presence and bestows a golden chain on the victor. But the very first man who wants that chain can dispute it with the wearer who, by having rid himself of one duel, finds himself with several more on his hands.

If we had thought that we had for ever overcome our enemy by valour and could dominate him as we pleased, we would be sorry indeed if he were to escape: he does that when he dies. We do want to beat him, but with more security than honour, and we seek not so much glory through our quarrel but the end of that quarrel.

For a man of honour Asinius Pollio also made a similar mistake: he wrote invectives against Plancus but waited until he died before he published them. That was like poking out your tongue to a blind man, shouting insults at a deaf one or hitting a man who cannot feel it, rather than risking his resentment. And they said of him that only the shades should shadow-box with the dead. Anyone who waits to see an author dead before attacking his writings, what does he reveal except that he is both weak and quarrelsome? Aristotle was told that someone had spoken ill of him: 'Let him do worse,' he replied, 'let him scourge me – as long as I am not there!'

Our fathers were content to avenge an insult by a denial; avenge a denial by a slap in the face; and so on in due order. They were valiant enough not to be afraid of an enemy who was outraged but living. We tremble with fear while we see him still on his feet. As proof of that, is it not one of our beautiful practices today to hound to death not only the man who has offended us but also the man we have offended?

It is also a reflection of our cowardice which has brought into our single combats the practice of our being accompanied by seconds – and thirds and fourths. Once upon a time there were duels: nowadays there are clashes and pitched battles. The first men who introduced such practices were afraid of acting on their own, '*cum in se cuique minimum fiduti æ esset*' [since neither had the slightest confidence in himself]. For it is natural that company of any sort brings comfort and solace in danger. Once upon a time there third parties were brought in to guard against rule-breaking and foul play and also to bear witness to the result of the duel; but now that it has come to such a pass that anyone who is invited along involves himself in the quarrel, he can no longer remain a spectator for fear that it was from lack of engagement or of courage. Apart from the injustice and baseness of such an action which engages in the defence of your honour some other might or valour than your own, I find it derogatory to anyone who does fully trust in himself to go and confound his fortune with that of another. Each of us runs risks enough for himself without doing so for another: each has enough to do to defend his life on behalf of his own valour without entrusting so dear a possession into the hands of third parties. For unless it be not expressly agreed to the contrary, the four of them form one party under bond. If your second is downed you are faced, by the rules, with two to contend with; you may say that that is unfair. And indeed it is – like charging well-armed against a man who has only the stump of his sword, or when you are still sound against a man who is already grievously wounded. However, when you have won such advantages in battle you can exploit them without dishonour. Inequality and disproportion weigh in our consideration only at the outset, when battle is joined: thereafter you can rail against Fortune! And even if you find yourself one against three after your two companions have been killed, they do you no more wrong than I would do if, in the wars with a similar advantage, I were to strike a blow with my sword at one of the enemy whom I found attacking one of our men. The nature of our alliances entails that when we have group against group (as when our Duke of Orleans challenged Henry, King of England, one hundred against one hundred; or three hundred against three hundred like the Argives against the Spartans; or three against three like the Horatii against the Curatii), whatever crowd there may be on either side they are regarded as one man. And whenever you have companions the chance of the outcome is confused and uncertain.

I have a private interest to declare in this discussion: for my brother the Seigneur de Matecoulom was summoned to Rome to act as second for a gentleman he hardly knew, who was the defender, having been challenged by another. By chance he found himself face to face with a man who was closer and better known to him (I would like to see somebody justify these 'laws of honour' which are so often opposed in hostility to the laws of reason). Having dispatched his opponent and seeing the two principals in the quarrel still unharmed on their feet, he went to the relief of his companion. What less could he do? Ought he to have remained quiet and watched the man defeated, if such was his lot, for whose defence he had come to Rome? All he had achieved so far was of no avail: the quarrel had still to be decided. The courtesy which you yourself can and must show to your enemy when you have reduced him to a sorry state and have him at a great disadvantage, I cannot see how you can show it when it concerns somebody else, when you are but the second, when the quarrel is not yours. He could neither be just nor courteous at the expense of the one to whom he had lent his support. So he was released from prison in Italy by the swift formal request of our King.

What a stupid nation we are. We are not content with letting the world know of our vices and follies by repute, we go to foreign nations in order to show them to them by our presence! Put three Frenchmen in the Libyan deserts and they will not be together for a month without provoking and clawing each other: you would say that one of the aims of these journeys is expressly to make spectacles of ourselves before foreigners – especially those who take delight in our misfortunes and laugh at them.

We go to Italy to learn fencing, and then put it into practice at the expense of our lives before we have learnt how. Yet, by the rules of instruction, theory should come before practice: we betray that we are mere apprentices:

> *Primitica juvenum miseræ, bellique futuri*
> *Dura rudimenta.*
> [Wretched first fruits of mere youth: harsh training for the future wars.]

I know that fencing is an art which achieves what it sets out to do: in the duel in Spain between two Princes who were German cousins, the elder, says Livy, easily overcame the reckless force of the younger by strategy and skill with his weapons. And as I myself know from experience it is an art which has raised the hearts of some above their natural measure; yet that is not really valour since it draws its support from skill and has some other foundation than itself. The honour of combat consists in rivalry of heart not of expertise; that is why I have seen some of my friends who are past masters in that exercise choosing for their duels weapons which deprived them of the means of exploiting their advantage and which depend entirely on fortune and steadfastness, so that nobody could attribute their victory to their fencing rather than to their valour. When I was a boy noblemen rejected a reputation for fencing as being an insult; they learned to fence in secret as some cunning craft which derogated from true inborn virtue:

> *Non schivar, non parar, non ritirarsi*
> *Voglion costor, ne qui destrezza ha parte.*
> *Non danno i colpi finti, hor pieni, hor scarsi:*
> *Toglie l'ira e il furor l'uso de l'arte.*
> *Odi le spade horribilmente urtarsi*
> *A mezzo il ferro; il pie d'orma non parte:*
> *Sempre è il pie fermo, è la man sempre in moto;*
> *Ne scende taglio in van, ne punta à voto.*
> [They have no wish to dodge, to parry nor to make tactical retreats: skill has no part to play in their encounter; they make no feints, nor blows oblique, nor shamming lunges; anger and fury strips them of their art. Just listen to the terrifying clash of striking swords, iron against iron; no foot gives way but stays ever planted firm: it is their arms which move; every thrust strikes home and no blows fall in vain.]

Our forebears' training was a true image of martial combat: target-practice, tournaments and the tilting-yard; that other skill is all the more ignoble in that it has nothing but a private end, teaching us to destroy each other against all law and justice and, whatever

102

else happens, always producing harmful effects. It is much more meet and right to practise such arts as defend our polity not those which undermine it, such as have regard for national security and the glory of the common weal.

Publius Rutilius when consul was the first to train soldiers in handling their weapons with skill and technique and to couple art and valour: but that was for the wars and contentions of the Roman People – official fencing for citizens in common. And, leaving aside Caesar's example when he ordered his men to aim principally at the faces of Pompey's men during the battle of Pharsalia, hundreds of other leaders of men in war have decided to employ new kinds of weapons and new ways of attack and defence according to the exigencies of the moment. But just as Philopoemen condemned wrestling (in which he excelled) because the basic skills learned in that sport were quite different from those which appertain to military training on which alone he reckoned that men of honour should spend their time, it seems to me also that those feints and tricks and that agility which young men acquire for their limbs in this new-fangled school are not merely useless for fighting wars but are hostile and harmful to it. Moreover people today normally use special weapons, specifically destined for fencing; I have noticed that it is hardly considered proper that a gentleman challenged to sword and dagger should turn up armed like a soldier.

It is worth considering that in Plato, Laches, talking about a kind of apprenticeship in weapon-training just like ours today, says that he has never seen any great soldier come out of such a school – and especially not from among the instructors! (As for that lot, our own experience teaches us the same!) We can also certainly at least assert that we are dealing with accomplishments which are quite unrelated and distinct. And in this system of education for the boys of his Republic Plato forbids fisticuffs (which was introduced by Amycus and Epeius) as well as wrestling (introduced by Antaeus and Cercyo) since they have some other aim than rendering youth more apt for service in war and contribute nothing to it. But I am wandering away from my theme.

The Emperor Maurice, having been warned by his dreams and several omens that he was to be killed by a certain Phocas, a soldier then unknown to him, inquired of his son-in-law Philip who this Phocas was, what he was like and how he behaved; when Philip told him that Phocas was among other things cowardly and fearful, the Emperor straightway concluded from this that he was therefore murderous and cruel. What is it that makes tyrants so lust for blood? It is their worries about their own safety and the fact that when they fear a scratch their cowardly minds can furnish them with no other means of security save exterminating all those who simply have the means of hurting them, women included.

Cuncta ferit, dum cuncta timet.
[Fearing all, he strikes at all.]

The first acts of cruelty are done for their own sake; from them there is born fear of a just revenge; that produces a succession of fresh cruelties, each intended to smother each other. Philip, King of Macedon, who had many a crossed thread to untangle with the Roman People, was shaken with terror by the murders committed on his orders; since he could not find a means of delivering himself from so many families harmed at various times, he decided to seize all the children of those he had put to death so as to kill them off, one by one, day after day . . . and so find rest.

Beautiful topics can always hold their own, no matter where you strew them. I who am more concerned with the weight and usefulness of my writings than with their order and logical succession must not be afraid to place here, a little off the track, an account of great beauty. Among the others condemned by Philip there was a certain Herodicus, Prince of the Thessalians. After him it was the turn of his two sons-in-law to be killed, each leaving a baby son. Their widows were called Theoxena and Archo. Theoxena was much courted but could not be brought to remarry. Archo married the leading man among the Aenians called Poris and had a number of sons by him who were all young when she died. Theoxena, feeling the urge to mother her nephews, wedded Poris. Then the King's edict was proclaimed. That courageous mother, fearing both the cruelty of Philip and the abusive lust of his underlings, boldly stated that she would kill them with her own hands rather than hand them over. Poris was terrified by this declaration of hers and promised to steal secretly away with them to Athens and place them under the protection of some of his faithful vassals. Taking advantage of a yearly feast celebrated in Aenia in honour of Aeneas, they set about it. After being present during the daytime at the ceremonies and the public banquet, they slipped away by night to a ship which was waiting to put some space between them. But there was a contrary wind; the following morning they were still in sight of the land where they had left their moorings and were pursued by the harbour-guards. When they were overhauled, while Poris was busy urging the sailors to flee faster Theoxena, raving mad with love for the children and for vengeance, returned to her original plan; she got weapons and poison ready; she then showed them to them saying, 'Come now, my children; from henceforth death is your sole means of defence and of remaining free; and it will provide the gods with something to work their hallowed justice upon. These drawn swords and these goblets open the way to it for you. Be brave. And you, my oldest son, grasp this blade and die the bolder death.' The children, with this staunch counsellor on one side and the enemy at their throats on the other, frantically ran to whatever goblet was nearest to hand

and were thrown still half-dead into the sea. Theoxena, proud of having so gloriously saved all her children, threw her arms passionately round her husband and said, 'Let us follow these boys, my love, and let us enjoy the same grave with them.' Clasped thus in each other's embrace, they plunged headlong into the sea. And so that boat was brought back to land empty of its masters.

Tyrants, to do two things at once (killing, and making their anger felt), have exhausted their ingenuity in inventing means of prolonging the death. They want to do in their enemies all right, but not so quickly that they have no time to spare for savouring their vengeance. In this they are greatly perplexed; for if the tortures are intense they are short: if they are long they are not painful enough to their liking; so they have to tread carefully with machinery of torture.

We can see hundreds of examples of this in Antiquity – and I wonder whether we do not still retain traces of such barbarity without our realising it. Everything which goes beyond mere death seems to me to be cruelty. Our justice cannot hope that a man who will not be kept from wrongdoing by fear of death on the block or the gallows may yet be deterred by the thought of pincers or a slow fire or the racking-wheel. And for all I know, during this time we drive them to despair: for in what state can a man's soul be as he lies waiting for death for twenty-four hours, broken on the wheel, or in the Ancient fashion nailed to a cross? Josephus relates how, during the Roman wars in Judaea, he was passing by the place where some Jews had been crucified three days before, when he recognised three of his friends and was allowed to take them away. 'Two of them died,' he says, 'and the other is still alive.'

Chalcocondylas, a reliable man, left memoirs of events which happened in his own time and near where he was; in them he relates as the ultimate in punishments the practice of the Emperor Mahomet who, with one blow from a scimitar, often had men sliced in two through their middle just above the abdomen so that they died as it were two deaths at once; 'And,' he adds, 'you could see both parts, still alive long afterwards, twitching and writhing in torment.' I am not convinced that those twitchings imply much pain. Tortures which are most ghastly to see are not always the harshest to suffer. More atrocious I find are the accounts in other historians of what he did to some of the noblemen of Epirus: he had them flayed alive, bit by bit, following a procedure so evilly devised that, for a whole fortnight, they lived to endure such anguish.

And there are those two others as well: Croesus, having seized one of his brother's intimate supporters called Pantaleon, dragged him off to a wool-carder's shop where he had him so excoriated with the carder's combs and teasels that he died from it; George Sechel (the leader of those Polish peasants who wrought such havoc under the pretext of a Crusade) was defeated and captured in battle by the Voivode of Transylvania;

he was strapped for three days, naked, to a wooden rack and subjected to every kind of torture which anyone at all could devise for him. During this time the other prisoners were given neither food nor drink. In the end, while he was still alive and able to see it, they compelled his dear brother Lucat to quench his thirst in his blood (but he went on praying for Lucat's safety, taking upon himself all the hatred aroused by their crimes); then they made twenty of his most intimate captains eat him, tearing at his flesh with their bare teeth and swallowing it down. Once he was dead they boiled his remaining flesh and entrails and gave it to others of his followers to eat.

– On Three Kinds of
Social Intercourse –

W e should not nail ourselves so strongly to our humours and complexions. Our main talent lies in knowing how to adapt ourselves to a variety of customs. To keep ourselves bound by the bonds of necessity to one single way of life is to be, but not to live. Souls are most beautiful when they show most variety and flexibility. Here is a testimony which honours Cato the Elder: '*Huic versatile ingenium sic pariter ad omnia fuit, ut natum ad id unum diceres, quodcumque ageret.*' [His mind was so versatile, and so ready for anything, that whatever he did you could say he was born for that alone.]

If it was for me to train myself my way, there would be no mould in which I would wish to be set without being able to throw it off. Life is a rough, irregular progress with a multitude of forms. It is to be no friend of yourself – and even less master of yourself – to be a slave endlessly following yourself, so beholden to your predispositions that you cannot stray from them nor bend them. I am saying this now because I cannot easily escape from the state of my own Soul, which is distressing in so far as she does not usually know how to spend her time without getting bogged down nor how to apply herself to anything except fully and intensely. No matter how trivial the subject you give her she likes to magnify it and to amplify it until she has to work at it with all her might. For this reason her idleness is an activity which is painful to me and which damages my health. Most minds have need of extraneous matter to make them limber up and do their exercises: mine needs rather to sojourn and to settle down: '*Vitia otii negotio discutienda sunt*' [We must dispel the vices of leisure by our work]; my own mind's principal and most difficult study is the study of itself. For it, books are the sort of occupation which seduces it from such study. With the first thoughts which occur to it it becomes agitated and makes a trial of its strength in all directions, practising its control, sometimes in the direction of force, sometimes in the direction of order and gracefulness, controlling, moderating and fortifying itself. It has the wherewithal to awaken its faculties by itself: Nature has given it (as she has given them all) enough matter of its own for its use and enough subjects for it to discover and pass judgement upon.

For anyone who knows how to probe himself and to do so vigorously, reflection is a mighty endeavour and a full one: I would rather forge my soul than stock it up. No occupation is more powerful, or more feeble, than entertaining one's own thoughts – depending on what kind of soul it is. The greatest of souls make it their vocation, '*quibus vivere est cogitare*' [for them, to think is to live]; there is nothing we can do longer than think, no activity to which we can devote ourselves more regularly nor more easily: Nature has granted the soul that prerogative. It is the work of the gods, says Aristotle, from which springs their beatitude and our own. Reading, by its various subjects, particularly serves to arouse my discursive reason: it sets not my memory to work but my judgement. So, for me, few conversations are arresting unless they are vigorous and powerful. It is true that grace and beauty occupy me and fulfil me as much or more as weight and profundity. And since I doze off during any sort of converse and lend it only the outer bark of my attention, it often happens that during polite conversation (with its flat, well-trodden sort of topics) I say stupid things unworthy of a child, or make silly, ridiculous answers, or else I remain stubbornly silent which is even more inept and rude. I have a mad way of withdrawing into myself as well as a heavy, puerile ignorance of everyday matters. To those two qualities I owe the fact that five or six true anecdotes can be told about me as absurd as about any man whatsoever.

Now to get on with what I was saying: this awkward complexion of mine renders me fastidious about mixing with people: I need to handpick my companions; and it also renders me awkward for ordinary activities. We live and deal with the common people; if their commerce wearies us, if we disdain to apply ourselves to their humble, common souls – and the humble, common ones are often as well-governed as the most refined (all wisdom being insipid which does not adapt to the common silliness) – then we must stop dealing with our own affairs and anyone else's: both public and personal business involves us with such people. The most beautiful motions of our soul are those which are least tense and most natural: and the best of its occupations are the least forced. O God! What good offices does Wisdom do for those whose desires she ranges within their powers! No knowledge is more useful. 'According as you can' was the refrain and favourite saying of Socrates, a saying of great substance. We must direct our desires and settle them on the things which are easiest and nearest. Is it not an absurd humour for me to be out of harmony with the hundreds of men to whom my destiny joins me and whom I cannot manage without, in order to restrict myself to one or two people who are beyond my ken? Or is it not rather a mad desire for something I cannot get?

My mild manners, which are the enemies of all sharpness and contentiousness, may easily have freed me from the burden of envy and unfriendliness: never did man give more occasion – I do not say to be loved but certainly not to be hated? But the lack of warmth in my converse has rightly robbed me of the good-will of many, who can be excused for interpreting it differently, in a worse sense.

Most of all I am able to make and keep exceptional and considered friendships, especially since I seize hungrily upon any acquaintanceship which corresponds to my tastes. I put myself forward and throw myself into them so eagerly that I can hardly fail to make attachments and to leave my mark wherever I go. I have often had a happy experience of this. In commonplace friendships I am rather barren and cold, for it is not natural to me to proceed except under full sail. Besides, the fact that as a young man I was brought to appreciate the delicious savour of one single perfect friendship has genuinely made the others insipid to me and impressed on my faculty of perception that (as one ancient writer said) friendship is a companiable, not a gregarious, beast. I also, by nature, find it hard to impart myself by halves, with limitations and with that suspicious vassal-like prudence prescribed to us for our commerce with those multiple and imperfect friendships – prescribed in our time above all, when you cannot talk to the world in general except dangerously or falsely.

Yet I can clearly see that anyone like me whose aim is the good things of life (I mean those things which are of its essence) must flee like the plague from such moroseness and niceness of humour. What I would praise would be a soul with many storeys, one of which knew how to strain and relax; a soul at ease wherever fortune led it; which could chat with a neighbour about whatever he is building, his hunting or his legal action, and take pleasure in conversing with a carpenter or a gardener. I envy those who can come down to the level of the meanest on their staff and make conversation with their own servants. I have never liked Plato's advice to talk always like a master to our domestics, without jests or intimacy, whether addressing menservants or maidservants. For, apart from what my own reason tells me, it is ill-bred and unjust to give such value to a trivial privilege of Fortune: the most equitable polities seem to me to be those which allow the least inequality between servants and masters.

Other men study themselves in order to wind their minds high and send them forth: I do so in order to bring mine lower and lay it down. It is vitiated only when it reaches out:

> *Narras, et genus Æaci,*
> *Et pugnata sacro bella sub Ilio:*
> *Quo Chium pretio cadum*
> *Mercemur, quis aquam temperet ignibus,*
> *Quo præbente domum, et quota,*
> *Pelignis caream frigoribus, taces.*
> [You sing of Aeacus' line and the wars beneath the sacred walls of Ilium: but you do not say how much I must pay for a jar of Chian wine, who will heat my water on his fire, where I shall find shelter and when I shall escape from the cold of the Pelignian mountains.]

Thus, just as Spartan valour needed moderating by the gentle gracious playing of flutes to calm it down in war lest it cast itself into rashness and frenzy (whereas all other peoples normally employ shrill sounds and powerful voices to stir and inflame the hearts of their warriors), so it seems to me that, in exercising our minds, we for the most part – contrary to normal practice – have greater need of lead-weights than of wings, of cold repose rather than hot agitation.

Above all, to my mind, it is to act like a fool to claim to be in the know amidst those who are not, and to be ever speaking guardedly – '*favellar in punta di forchetta*' [speaking daintily, 'with the prongs of your fork']. You must come down to the level of those you are with, sometimes even affecting ignorance. Thrust forceful words and subtleties aside: when dealing with ordinary folk it is enough if you maintain due order. Meanwhile, if they want you to, creep along at ground-level. That is the stone which scholars frequently trip up over. They are always parading their mastery of their subject and scattering broadcast whatever they have read. Nowadays they have funnelled so much of it into the ears of the ladies in their drawing-rooms that, even though those ladies of ours have retained none of the substance, they look as though they have: on all sorts of topics and subjects, no matter how menial or commonplace, they employ a style of speaking and writing which is newfangled and erudite:

> *Hoc sermone pavent, hoc iram, gaudia, curas,*
> *Hoc cuncta effundunt animi secreta; quid ultra?*
> *Concumbunt docte.*
> [This is the style in which they express their fears, their anger, their joy and their cares. This is the style in which they pour forth all their secrets; why, they even lie with you eruditely.]

They cite Plato and St Thomas Aquinas for things which the first passer-by could serve to support. That doctrine which they have learned could not reach their minds so it has stayed on their tongues. However well-endowed they are, they will, if they trust me, be content to make us value the natural riches proper to them. They hide and drape their own beauties under borrowed ones. There is great simpleness in such smothering of their own light so as to shine with borrowed rays; they are dead and buried under artifice: '*De capsula totae.*' [All out of the clothes-press.]

That is because they do not know enough about themselves: there is nothing in the whole world as beautiful; they it is who should be lending honour to art and beauty to cosmetics. What more do they want than to live loved and honoured? They have enough, and know enough, to do that. All that is needed is a little arousing and enhancing of the qualities which are in them. When I see them saddled with rhetoric, judicial astrology, logic and such-like vain and useless trash, I begin to fear that the men who counsel them to do so see it as a way of having a pretext for manipulating them. For what other excuse can I find for them?

It suffices that ladies (without our having to tell them how) can attune the grace of their eyes to gaiety, severity and gentleness; season. 'No! No!' with rigour, doubt or favour; and seek no hidden meanings in the speeches with which we court them. With knowledge like that it is they who wield the big stick and dominate the dominies and their schools.

Should it nevertheless irk them to lag behind us in anything whatsoever; should they want a share in our books out of curiosity: then poetry is a pastime rightly suited to their needs: it is a frivolous, subtle art, all disguise and chatter and pleasure and show, like they are. They will also draw a variety of benefits from history; and in philosophy – the part which helps us to live well – they will find such arguments as train them to judge of our humours and our attributes, to shield them from our deceptions, to control the rashness of their own desires, to cultivate their freedom and prolong the pleasure of this life, and to bear with human dignity the inconstancy of a suitor, the moroseness of a husband and the distress of wrinkles and the passing years. That sort of thing.

That – at most – is the share of learning that I would assign to them.

Some natures are withdrawn, enclosed and private. The proper essence of my own form lies in imparting things and in putting them forth: I am all in evidence; all of me is exposed; I was born for company and loving relationships. The solitude which I advocate is, above all, nothing but the bringing of my emotions and thoughts back to myself, restricting and restraining not my wandering footsteps but my anxiety and my desires, abandoning disquiet about external things and fleeing like death from all slavery and obligation, and running away not so much from the throng of people as from the throng of affairs.

To tell the truth, localised solitude makes me reach out and extend myself more: I throw myself into matters of State and into the whole universe more willingly when I am alone. In a crowd at the Louvre I hold back and withdraw into my skin; crowds drive me back into myself and my thoughts are never more full of folly, more licentious and private than in places dedicated to circumspection and formal prudence. It is not our folly which makes me laugh: it is our wisdom.

I am not by complexion hostile to the jostlings of the court: I have spent part of my life there and am so made that I can be happy in large groups provided that it be at intervals and at my own choosing. But that lax judgement I am speaking of forces me to bind myself to solitude even in my own home, in the midst of a crowded household which is among the most visited. I meet plenty of people there, but rarely those whom I love to converse with; and I reserve an unusual degree of liberty there for myself and for others. There we have called a truce with all etiquette, welcomings and escortings and other such painful practices decreed by formal courtesy. (Oh what servile and distressing customs!) Everybody goes his own way; anyone who wants to can think his own thoughts: I remain dumb, abstracted and inward-looking – no offence to my guests.

I am seeking the companionship and society of such men as we call honourable and talented: my ideal of those men makes me lose all taste for the others. It is, when you reflect on it, the rarest of all our forms; and it is a form which is mainly owed to nature. The ends of intercourse with such men are simply intimacy, the frequenting of each other and discussion – exercising our souls with no other gain. In our conversation any topic will do: I do not worry if they lack depth or weight: there is always the grace and the appropriateness: everything in it is coloured by ripe and sustained judgement mingled with frankness, goodwill, gaiety and affection. Our minds do not merely show their force and beauty on the subject of entailed property or our kings' business: they show it just as well in our private discussions together. I recognise my kind of men by their very silences or their smiles; and I perhaps discover them better at table than in their workrooms. Hippomachus said that he could tell a good wrestler simply by seeing him walk down the street.

If Erudition wants to mingle in our discussions, then she will not be rejected, though she must not be, as she usually is, professorial, imperious and unmannerly, but courting approval, herself ready to learn. We are merely seeking a pastime: when the time comes to be lectured to and preached at we will go and seek her on her throne. Let her be kind enough to come down to us on this occasion, please! For, useful and desirable as she is, I presume that if we had to we could get on quite well in her absence and achieve our effect without her. A well-endowed Soul, used to dealing with

men, spontaneously makes herself totally agreeable.
Art is but the register and accounts of the products of
such souls.

There is for me another delightful kind of converse: that with beautiful and honourable women:
'*Nam nos quoque oculos eruditos habemus.*' [For we too
have well-taught eyes.] Though there is less here for
our souls to enjoy than in the first kind, our physical
senses, which play a greater part in this one, restore
things to a proportion very near to the other – though
for me not an equal one. But it is a commerce where
we should remain a bit on our guard, especially men
like me over whom the body has a lot of power. I was
scalded once or twice in my youth and suffered all the
ragings which the poets say befall men who inordinate-
ly and without judgement let go of themselves in such
matters. It is true that I got a beating which taught me
a lesson:

> *Quicunque Argolica de classe Capharea fugit,*
> *Semper ab Euboicis vela retorquet aquis.*
> [Anyone in the Grecian fleet who escaped from that
> shipwreck on the promontory of Caphareus ever there-
> after turns his sails away from the waters of Euboea.]

It is madness to fix all our thoughts on it and to engage in it with a frenzied singleminded passion. On the
other hand to get involved in it without love or willing
to be bound, like actors, so as to play the usual part

expected from youth, contributing nothing of your own but your words, is indeed to provide for your safety; but it is very cowardly, like a man who would jettison his honour, goods and pleasure from fear of danger. For one thing is certain: those who set such a snare can expect to gain nothing by it which can affect or satisfy a soul of any beauty. We must truly have desired any woman we wish truly to enjoy possessing; I mean that, even though fortune should unjustly favour play-acting – as often happens, since there is not one woman, no matter how ugly she may be, who does not think herself worth loving and who does not think herself attractive for her laugh, her gestures or for being the right age, since none of them is universally ugly any more than universally beautiful. (When the daughters of the Brahmans have nothing else to commend them, the town-crier calls the people together in the market-place expressly for them to show off their organs of matrimony to see whether they at least can be worth a husband to them.) It follows that there is not one who fails to let herself be convinced by the first oath of devotion sworn by her suitor. Now from the regular routine treachery of men nowadays there necessarily results what experience already shows us: to escape us, women turn in on themselves and have recourse to themselves or to other women; or else they, on their side, follow the example we give them, play their part in the farce and join in the business without passion concern or love. '*Neque affectui suo aut alieno obnoxiae*'

[Beholden to no love, their own or anyone else's]; following the conviction of Lysias in Plato and reckoning that the less we love them the more usefully and agreeably they can devote themselves to it. It will go as in comedies: the audience will have as much pleasure as the comedians, or more.

As for me, I no more know Venus without Cupid than motherhood without children: they are things whose essences are interdependent and necessary to each other. So such cheating splashes back on the man who does it. The *affaire* costs him hardly anything, but he gets nothing worthwhile out of it either.

Those who turned Venus into a goddess considered that her principal beauty was not a matter of the body but of the spirit: yet the 'beauty' such men are after is not simply not human, it is not even bestial. The very beasts do not desire it so gross and so earthbound: we can see that imagination and desire often set beasts on heat and arouse them before their body does; we can see that beasts of both sexes choose and select the object of their desires from among the herd and that they maintain long affectionate relationships. Even beasts which are denied physical powers by old age still quiver, whinny and tremble with love. We can see them full of hope and fire before copulation, and, once the body has played its part, still tickling themselves with the sweet memory of it; some we see which swell with pride as they make their departure and which produce songs of joy and triumph, being tired but satisfied. A beast which merely wished to discharge some natural necessity from its body would have no need to bother another beast with such careful preparations: we are not talking about feeding some gross and lumpish appetite.

Being a man who does not ask to be thought better than I am, I will say this about the errors of my youth: I rarely lent myself to venal commerce with prostitutes, not only because of the danger to my health (though even then I did not manage to escape a couple of light anticipatory doses) but also because I despised it. I wanted to sharpen the pleasure by difficulties, by yearning and by a kind of glory; I liked the style of the Emperor Tiberius (who in his love-affairs was attracted more by modesty and rank than by any other quality) and the humour of Flora the courtesan (who was also attracted by a dictator, a consul or censor, delighting in the official rank of her lovers). Pearls and brocade certainly add to the pleasure; so do titles and retainers. Moreover I set a high value on wit, provided however that the body was not wanting; for if one of those two qualities had to be lacking, I must admit in all conscience that I would have chosen to make do without the wit; it has use in better things. But where love is concerned – subject which is mainly connected with sight and touch – you can achieve something without the witty graces but nothing without the bodily ones.

Beauty is the true privilege of noblewomen. It is so

much more proper to them than ours is to us men, that even though ours requires slightly different traits, at its highest point it is boyish and beardless, and therefore confounded with theirs. They say that in the place of the Grand Seigneur males chosen to serve him for their beauty – and they are countless in number – are sent away at twenty-two at the latest. Reasoning powers, wisdom and the offices of loving-friendship are rather to be found in men: that is why they are in charge of world affairs.

Those two forms of converse depend on chance and on other people. The first is distressingly rare, the second withers with age, so they could not have adequately provided for the needs of my life. Converse with books (which is my third form) is more reliable and more properly our own. Other superior endowments it concedes to the first two: its own share consists in being constantly and easily available with its services. This converse is ever at my side throughout my life's course and is everywhere present. It consoles me in my old age and in my retreat; it relieves me of the weight of distressing idleness and, at any time, can rid me of boring company. It blunts the stabs of pain whenever the pain is not too masterful and extreme. To distract me from morose thought I simply need to have recourse to books; they can easily divert me to them and rob me of those thoughts. And yet there is no mutiny when they see that I only seek them for want of other benefits which are more real, more alive, more natural: they always welcome me with the same expression.

It is all very well, we say, for a man to go on foot when he leads a ready horse by the bridle! And our James, King of Naples, manifested a kind of austerity which was still delicate and vacillating, when, young, handsome and healthy, he had himself wheeled about the land on a bier, lying, on a cheap feather-pillow, clad in a robe of grey cloth with a bonnet to match, followed meanwhile by great regal pomp with all sorts of litters and horses to hand, and by officers and noblemen. 'No need to pity an invalid who has a remedy up his coat-sleeve!' All the profit which I draw from books consists in experiencing and applying that proverb (which is a very true one). In practice I hardly use them more than those who are quite unacquainted with them. I enjoy them as misers do riches: because I know I can always enjoy them whenever I please. My soul is satisfied and contented by this right of possession. In war as in peace I never travel without books. Yet days and even months on end may pass without my using them. 'I will read them soon,' I say, 'or to-morrow; or when I feel like it.' Thus the time speeds by and is gone, but does me no harm; for it is impossible to describe what comfort and peace I derive from the thought that they are there beside me, to give me pleasure whenever I want it, or from recognising how much succour they bring to my life. It is the best protection which I have found for our human journey and

I deeply pity men of intelligence who lack it. I on the other hand can accept any sort of pastime, no matter how trifling, because I have this one which will never fail me.

At home I slip off to my library a little more often; it is easy for me to oversee my household from there. I am above my gateway and have a view of my garden, my chicken-run, my backyard and most parts of my house. There I can turn over the leaves of this book or that, a bit at a time without order or design. Sometimes my mind wanders off, at others I walk to and fro, noting down and dictating these whims of mine.

It is on the third storey of a tower. The first constitutes my chapel; the second, a bed-chamber with a dressing-room, where I often sleep when I want to be alone. Above that there is a large drawing-room. It was formerly the most useless place in my house: I spend most days of my life there, and most hours of each day, but I am never there at night. It leads on to quite an elegant little chamber which can take a fire in winter and agreeably lets in the light. If I feared the bother as little as the expense – and the bother drives me away from any task – I could erect a level gallery on either side, a hundred yards long and twelve yards wide, having found all the walls built (for some other purpose) at the required height. Every place of retreat needs an ambulatory. My thoughts doze off if I squat them down. My wit will not budge if my legs are not moving – which applies to all who study without books.

My library is round in shape, squared off only for the needs of my table and chair; as it curves round it offers me at a glance every one of my books ranged on five shelves all the way along. It has three splendid and unhampered views and a circle of free space sixteen yards in diameter. I am less continuously there in winter since my house is perched on a hill (hence its name) and no part of it is more exposed to the wind than that one. By being rather hard to get at and a bit out of the way it pleases me, partly for the sake of the exercise and partly because it keeps the crowd from me. There I have my seat. I assay making my dominion over it absolutely pure, withdrawing this one corner from all intercourse, filial, conjugal and civic. Everywhere else I have but a verbal authority, one essentially impure. Wretched the man (to my taste) who has nowhere in his house where he can be by himself, pay court to himself in private and hide away! Ambition well rewards its courtiers by keeping them always on display like a statue in the market-place: '*Magna servitus est magna fortuna.*' [A great destiny is great slavery.] They cannot even find privacy on their privy! I have never considered any of the austerities of life which our monks delight in to be harsher than the rule that I have noted in some of their foundations: to be perpetually with somebody else and to be surrounded by a crowd of people no matter what they are doing. And I find that it is somewhat more tolerable to be always alone than never able to be so.

If anyone says to me that to use the Muses as mere playthings and pastimes is to debase them, then he does not know as I do the value of pleasure, plaything or pastime. I could almost say that any other end is laughable. I live from day to day; and, saving your reverence, I live only for myself. My plans stop there. In youth I studied in order to show off; later, a little, to make myself wiser; now I do it for amusement, never for profit. A silly spendthrift humour that once I had for furnishing myself with books, not to provide for my needs but three paces beyond that, so as to paper my walls with them as decorations, I gave up long ago.

Books have plenty of pleasant qualities for those who know how to select them. But there is no good without ill. The pleasure we take in them is no purer or untarnished than any other. Reading has its disadvantages – and they are weighty ones: it exercises the soul, but during that time the body (my care for which I have not forgotten) remains inactive and grows earthbound and sad. I know of no excess more harmful to me in my declining years, nor more to be avoided.

There you have my three favourite private occupations. I make no mention of the ones I owe to the world through my obligations to the state.

– On Diversion –

Once I was charged with consoling a lady who was feeling distress – genuinely (mostly their mourning is affected and ritualistic):

> *Uberibus semper lachrimis, semperque paratis*
> *In statione sua, atque expectantibus illam,*
> *Quo jubeat manare modo.*
> [A woman has a reserve of abundant tears ever ready to flow, ever awaiting her decision to make them do so.]

To oppose such suffering is the wrong way to proceed, for opposition goads the women on and involves them more deeply in their sadness; zeal for argument makes a bad condition worse. (We can see that from commonplace discussions: if anyone challenges some casual statement of mine I become all formal and wedded to it; more so if it is a matter of concern to me.) And then, by acting that way you set about your cure in a rough manner, whereas the first greetings which a doctor makes to his patient must be cheerful, pleasing and full of grace: nothing was ever achieved by an ugly uncouth doctor. So from the outset you must, on the contrary, encourage women's lamentations and show that

they are justified and have your approval. This understanding between you will earn you the trust needed to
proceed further; then you can glide down an easy and
imperceptible slope to the more steadfast arguments
appropriate for curing them. Personally, since my main
desire was to escape from the bystanders who all kept
their eyes on me, I decided in this difficult case to plaster over the cracks. And so I found out by experience
that when it came to persuasion I was unsuccessful and
heavy-handed: I either offer my arguments too point-
edly and drily or else too brusquely, showing too little concern. After I had sympathised with her anguish
for a while, I made no assay at curing it by powerful
vigorous arguments (because I never had any, or perhaps because I thought I could achieve my effect better by another way); and I did not start choosing any
of the various methods which philosophy prescribes
for consoling grief, saying like Cleanthes for example
that what we are lamenting is not an evil; nor did I
say like the Peripatetics that it is but a light one; nor
like Chrysippus that such plaints are neither just nor
laudable; nor did I follow Epicurus' remedy (which is
close neighbour to my own), that of shifting her mind
away from painful thoughts to pleasant ones; nor did I
attack her grief with the weight of all those arguments
put together, dispensing them as required like Cicero:
but by gently deflecting our conversation and gradually leading it on to the nearest subject, and then on
to slightly more remote ones depending on how she

answered me, I imperceptibly stole her from her pain-ful thoughts; and as long as I remained with her I kept her composed and totally calm.

I made use of a diversion. But those who came to help her after me found no improvement in her, since I had not set my axe to the root of the trouble.

I have doubtless touched elsewhere on the kind of diversion used in politics. And the practice of military diversions (such as those used by Pericles in the Pelo-ponnesian Wars and by hundreds of others in order to tempt the enemy forces from their lands) is very com-mon in the history books.

It was an ingenious diversion by which the Sieur de Himbercourt saved himself and others in the town of Liège, which the Duke of Burgundy, who was be-sieging it, had obliged him to enter so as to draw up agreed terms of surrender. The citizens assembled for this purpose by night but began to rebel against what had previously been agreed; several decided to fall upon the negotiators whom they had in their power. He heard the rumble of the first wave of citizens who were coming to break into his apartments, so he at once dispatched two of the inhabitants – there were several with him – bearing new and milder conditions to put before their town council; he had made them up for the occasion, then and there. These two men calmed the original storm and led that excited mob to the Hôtel de Ville to hear the terms they were charged with and to deliberate upon them. The deliberation was brief; whereupon a second storm was unleashed, as animated as the first; so he dispatched four new mediators similar to the first two, protesting that he now wanted to announce much more tempting conditions which would entirely please and satisfy them; by this means he drove the citizens back to their conclave. In short, by managing to waste their time that way he diverted their frenzy, dissipated it in vain deliberations and eventually lulled it to sleep until daybreak – which had been his main concern.

My next story is in the same category. Atalanta was a maiden of outstanding beauty and wonderfully fleet of foot; to rid herself of a crowd of a thousand suitors all seeking to wed her, she decreed that she would accept the one who could run a race as fast as she could, provided that all those who failed should lose their lives. There were found plenty who reckoned the prize worth the hazard and who incurred the penalty of that cruel bargain. Hippomenes' turn to make an assay came after the others; he besought the goddess who protects all amorous passion to come to his aid. She answered his prayer by furnishing him with three golden apples and instructing him in their use. As the race was being run, when Hippomenes felt his lady pressing hard on his heels he dropped one of the apples as though inadvertently. The maiden was arrested by its beauty and did not fail to turn aside to pick it up.

Obstupuit virgo, nitidique cupidine pomi
Delinat cursus, aurumque volubile tollit.
[The maiden was seized by ecstasy and desire for the
smooth apple: she turns from the race and picks up the
golden ball as it rolls along.]

At the right moment he did the same with the second
and the third apples, finally winning the race because
of those distractions and diversions.

When our doctors cannot purge a catarrh they divert it towards another part of us where it can do less
harm. I have noticed that to be also the most usual prescription for illnesses of our soul: '*Abducendus etiam*
non-nunquam animus est ad alia studia, solicitudines, cu-
ras, negotia; loci denique mutatione, tanquam ægroti non
convalescentes, sæpe curandus est.' [The mind is often
to be deflected towards other anxieties, worries, cares
and occupations; and finally it is often cured (like the
sick when slow to recover) by a change of place.] Doctors can rarely get the soul to mount a direct attack on
her illness: they make her neither withstand the attack
nor beat it off, parrying it rather and diverting it.

The next example is too grand and too difficult;
only the highest category of men can stop to take a
pure look at the phenomenon itself, reflecting on it
and judging it. It behoves none but Socrates to greet
death with a normal countenance, training himself for
it and sporting with it. He seeks no consolation not
inherent to the deed: dying seems to him a natural

and neutral event; he justly fixes his gaze upon it and, without looking elsewhere, is resolved to accept it. Whereas the disciples of Hegesias (who were excited by his beautiful discourses during his lectures and who starved themselves to death in such quantities that King Ptolemy forbade him to defend such murderous doctrines in his School) were not considering the dying as such and were definitely not making a judgement about it; it was not on dying that they fixed their thoughts: they had a new existence in view and were dashing to it. Those poor wretches to be seen on our scaffolds, filled with a burning zeal to which they devote, as far as they are able, all their senses – their ears drinking in the exhortations they receive, while their arms and their eyes are lifted up to Heaven and their voices raised in loud prayer full of fierce and sustained emotion – are certainly performing a deed worthy of praise and proper to such an hour of need. We must praise them for their faith but not strictly for their constancy. They flee the struggle; they divert their thoughts from it (just as we occupy our children's attention when we want to use a lancet on them). Some I have seen occasionally lowering their gaze on to the horrifying preparations for their death which are all about them: then they fall into a trance and cast their frenzied thoughts elsewhere.

Those who have to cross over some terrifyingly deep abyss are told to close their eyes or to avert them.

On Nero's orders Subrius Flavius was condemned to be put to death at the hands of Niger. Both were military commanders. When he was escorted to the field of execution he saw that the grave which Niger had ordered to be dug for him was uneven and shoddily made; turning to the soldiers about him he snapped, 'You could not do even this according to your military training!' And when Niger urged him to keep his head straight, he retorted, 'I hope you can strike as straight!' And he guessed right: Niger's arms were all a-tremble and he needed several blows to chop his head off. Now there was a man who did fix his attention directly on the object.

A soldier who dies in the melee, his weapons in his hand, is not contemplating death: he neither thinks of it nor dwells on it; he is carried away by the heat of battle. An honourable man that I know was struck to the ground after entering the lists to do battle; while he was down he felt his enemy stab him nine or ten times with a dagger. Everybody present yelled at him to make peace with his conscience, but he told me later that although their words touched his ears they did not get through to him; he had no thought but of struggling loose and avenging himself; and he did kill his man in that very fight.

The soldier who brought news of his sentence to Lucius Silanus did him a great service; having heard Silanus reply that he was prepared to die but not at such wicked hands, the man rushed at him with his soldiers to take him by force, while he, all unarmed as he was, stoutly resisted with fists and feet. They killed him in the struggle. By his quick and stormy anger he destroyed the pain he would have felt from the long-drawn-out death awaiting him to which he had been destined.

Our thoughts are always elsewhere. The hope of a better life arrests us and comforts us; or else it is the valour of our sons or the future glory of our family-name, or an escape from the evils of this life or from the vengeance menacing those who are causing our death:

> *Spero equidem mediis, si quid pia numina possunt,*
> *Supplicia hausurum scopulis, et nomine Dido*
> *Sæpe vocaturum . . .*
> *Audiam, et hæc manes veniet mihi fama sub imos.*
> [I hope that if the righteous deities can prevail you will drink the cup of my vengeance, driven on the rocks in the midst of the sea, constantly crying out the name of Dido . . . I shall hear it, and its fame will reach me in the deepest Underworld.]

Crowned in the victor's garland Xenophon was performing his sacrificial rites when he was told of the death of Gryllus his son at the battle of Mantinea. His first reaction to this news was to throw down his gar-land; but then, when he heard of the very valorous style of his son's death, he picked it up from the ground and placed it back on his head.

.

When he was dying, even Epicurus found consolation in the eternity and moral usefulness of his writings: '*Omnes clari et nobilitati labores fiunt tolerabiles*' [All labours are bearable which bring fame and glory]; and (says Xenophon) the identical wound and travail do not grieve a General as much as an Other Rank. Epaminondas accepted death much more cheerfully for being told that his side was victorious. '*Haec sunt solatia, haec fomenta summorum dolorum.*' [Such things bring solace and comfort to the greatest of sufferings.]

Other similar circumstances can divert and distract us from considering the thing in itself. In fact the arguments of philosophy are constantly skirting the matter and dodging it, scarcely grazing the outer surface with its fingertips. The great Zeno, the leading figure in the leading school of philosophy which dominates all the others, says this concerning death: 'No evil is to be honoured; death is honoured: therefore death is no evil'; and he says of drunkenness, 'No one confides his secrets to a drunkard; each man trusts the wise man: therefore the wise man will not be a drunkard.' Do you call that hitting the bull's-eye! I delight in seeing those first-rate minds unable to free themselves from fellowship with the likes of us! Perfect men though they may be, they always remain grossly human.

Vengeance is a sweet passion deeply ingrained in us by our nature; I can see that clearly, even though I have never experienced it. Recently, having to draw a young prince away from it, I did not start by saying that when anyone strikes you on one cheek you must, as a work of charity, turn the other, nor did I draw a picture of the tragic results which poets attribute to that passion. I left vengeance aside and spent my time making him savour the beauty of the opposite picture: the honour, acclaim and goodwill he would acquire from clemency and bounty.

I diverted him towards ambition. That is how we get things done.

If when in love your passion is too powerful, dissipate it, they say. And they say truly: I have often usefully made the assay. Break it down into a variety of desires, one of which may rule as master if you like, but enfeeble it and delay it by subdividing it and diverting it, lest it dominate you and tyrannise over you:

> *Cum morosa vago singultiet inguine vena,*
> *Conjicito humorem collectum in corpora quæque.*
> [When the peevish vein gurgles in your vagrant groin,
> ejaculate the gathered fluid into any bodies whatever.]

And see to it quickly, lest you find yourself in trouble once it has seized hold of you,

> *Si non prima novis conturbes vulnera plagis,*
> *Volgivagaque vagus venere ante recentia cures*
> [unless you befuddle those first wounds by new ones,
> effacing the first by roaming as a rover through vagrant
> Venus.]

Once upon a time I was touched by a grief, powerful on account of my complexion and as justified as it was powerful. I might well have died from it if I had merely trusted to my own strength. I needed a mind-departing distraction to divert it; so by art and effort I made myself fall in love, helped in that by my youth. Love comforted me and took me away from the illness brought on by that loving-friendship. The same applies everywhere: some painful idea gets hold of me; I find it quicker to change it than to subdue it. If I cannot substitute an opposite one for it, I can at least find a different one. Change always solaces it, dissolves it and dispels it. If I cannot fight it, I flee it; and by my flight I made a diversion and use craft; by changing place, occupation and company I escape from it into the crowd of other pastimes and cogitations, in which it loses all track of me and cannot find me.

That is Nature's way when it grants us inconstancy; for Time, which she has given us as the sovereign doctor of our griefs, above all achieves its ends by furnishing our power of thought with ever more different concerns, so dissolving and breaking up the original concept however strong it may be. A wise man can see his dying friend scarcely less clearly after five-and-twenty years than after the first year, and according to Epicurus not a jot less, for he attributed no lessening of our sufferings either to our anticipating them or to their growing old. But so many other thoughts cut across the first one that in the end it grows tired and weary.

To change the direction of current gossip Alcibia-des lopped off the ears and tail of his beautiful dog and then chased it out into the square, so that by giving the populace something else to chatter about they would leave his other activities in peace. I have known wom-en too who have hidden their true affections under pretended ones, in order to divert people's opinions and conjectures and to mislead the gossips. But one I knew got well and truly caught: by feigning a passion, she quitted her original one for the feigned one. From her I learned that lovers who are well received ought not to consent to such mummery: sincc overt greetings and meetings are reserved for that decoy of a suitor, believe you me he will not be very clever if he does not eventually take your place and give you his. That really is cobbling and stitching a shoe for another to wear.

We can be distracted and diverted by small things, since small things are capable of holding us. We hardly ever look at great objects in isolation: it is the trivial circumstances, the surface images, which strike us – the useless skins which objects slough off,

> *Folliculos ut nunc teretes æstate cicadæ*
> *Linquunt.*
> [such as those smooth eggshells which the cicadas cast off in summer.]

Even Plutarch laments his daughter by recalling her babyish tricks as a child. We can be afflicted by the memory of a farewell, of a gesture of some special charm or a last request. Caesar's toga threw all Rome into turmoil – something which his death did not achieve. Take the forms of address which stay ringing in our ears – 'My poor Master'; or 'My dear friend'; or 'Dear papa' or 'My darling daughter': if I examine them closely when their repetition grips me, I discover that the grief lies in grammar and phonetics! What affects me are the words and the intonation (just as it is not the preacher's arguments which most often move a congregation but his interjections – like the pitiful cry of a beast being slaughtered for our use); during that time I cannot weigh the mass of my subject or penetrate to its real essence:

His se stimulis dolor ipse lacessit;
[With goads such as these grief wounds its own self;]

yet they are the foundations of our grief.

The stubborn nature of my stones, especially when in my prick, has sometimes forced me into prolonged suppressions of urine during three or four days; they bring me so far into death that, given the cruelty of the strain which that condition entails, it would have been madness to hope to avoid dying or even to want to do so. (Oh what a past master of the art of torment was that fair Emperor who used to bind his criminals' pricks and make them die for want of pissing!) Having got that far I would consider how light were the stimuli and the objects of my thought which could nurse a regret for life in me, and what minutiae served to construct in my soul the weight and difficulty of her departure; I would consider how frivolous are the images we find room for in so great a matter – a hound, a horse, a book, a wine-glass and what-not had their role in my loss. Others have their ambitious hopes, their money-bags or their erudition, which to my taste are no less silly. When I looked upon death as the end of my life, universally, then I looked upon it with indifference. Wholesale, I could master it: retail, it savaged me; the tears of a manservant, the distributing of my wardrobe, the known touch of a hand, a routine word of comfort discomforted me and made me weep.

In the same way we disturb our souls with fictional laments; the plaints of Dido and Ariadne in Virgil and Catullus arouse the feelings of the very people who do *not* believe in them. To experience no emotion from them is to be like Polemon (of whom that is told as a miracle) and to serve as an example of a hard and inflexible heart – but Polemon of course did not even blench when a mad dog chewed off his calf!

By inquiry no wisdom can draw so close towards understanding the condition of a living, total grief but that it will be drawn closer still by physical presence, when ears and eyes (organs which can be stirred by inessentials only) can play their part.

Is it right for the arts to profit from our feeble-mindedness and inborn stupidity? The orator (says

Rhetoric) when acting out his case will be moved by the sound of his own voice and by his own feigned indignation; he will allow himself to be taken in by the emotion he is portraying. By acting out his part as in a play he will stamp on himself the essence of true grief and then transmit it to the judges (who are even less involved in the case than he is); it is like those mourners who are rented for funerals and who sell their tears and grief by weight and measure: for even though they only borrow their signs of grief, it is nevertheless certain that by habitually adopting the right countenance they often get carried away and find room inside themselves for real melancholy.

With several other of his friends I once had to escort the body of the Sieur de Gramont from La Fère, where he was killed in the siege, to Soissons. I reflected that wherever we passed it was by the sheer display of the pomp of our procession that we filled the populace with tears and lamentations, since they had never even heard of his name!

Quintilian says that he had known actors to be so involved in playing the part of a mourner that they were still shedding tears after they had returned home; and of himself he says that, having accepted to arouse grief in somebody else, he had so wedded himself to that emotion that he found himself surprised not only by tears but by pallor of face and by the stoop of a man truly weighed down by grief.

In a country place hard by our mountains the

women play both priest and clerk, like Father Martin. They magnify their grief for their lost husbands by recalling their good and agreeable qualities but at the same time (to counterbalance this, it seems, and to divert their pitiful feelings towards contempt) they also list and proclaim all their failings – with far better grace than we have when we lose a mere acquaintance and pride ourselves on bestowing on him novel and fictitious praises, turning him, once he is lost to sight, into something quite different from what he appeared to be when we used to see him – as though regret taught us something new and tears could lave our minds and bring enlightenment to them. Here and now I renounce any flattering eulogies you may wish to make of me, not because I shall not have deserved them but because I shall then be dead!

If you ask that man over there, 'How does this siege concern you?' he will reply: 'I am concerned to give an example of routine obedience to my Prince; I do not expect to gain any benefit from it. And as for glory, I know what a small share of it can concern a private individual like me. I feel no passion; I make no claims.' Yet look at him the following morning; there he is, ready for the assault in his place in the ranks; he is entirely changed, boiling, flushed with yellow bile. What has sent this new determination and hatred coursing through his veins is the glint of so much steel, the flashes of our cannon and the din of our kettle-drums.

'A frivolous cause,' you will say. What do you mean, cause? To excite our souls we need no causes: they can be controlled and excited by some raving disembodied fancy based on nothing. When I throw myself into building castles in the air my imagination forges me pleasures and comforts which give *real* delight and joy to my soul. How often do we encumber our spirits with yellow bile or sadness by means of such shadows? And we put ourselves into fantastical rages, deleterious to our souls and bodies! What confused, ecstatic, madly laughing grimaces can be brought to our faces by such ravings! What jerkings of our limbs and trembling of our voices! That man over there is on his own, but does he not seem to be deceived by visions of a crowd of other men whom he has to deal with, or else to be persecuted by some devil within him?

Ask yourself where is the object which produced such an alteration: apart from us men, is there anything in nature which is sustained by inanities or over which they have such power? Cambyses dreamt in his sleep that his brother was to become King of Persia; so he killed him – a beloved brother whom he had always relied on! Aristodemus, King of the Messenians, on account of an idea put into his head of some ill omen read into the howling of his dogs, killed himself. King Midas did the same, disturbed and worried by some unpleasant dream he had had.

Abandoning your life for a dream is to value it for exactly what it is worth. Listen though to our soul triumphing over her wretched body and its frailty, as the butt of all indispositions and degradations. A fat lot of reason she has to talk!

> *O prima infælix fingenti terra Prometheo!*
> *Ille parum cauti pectoris egit opus.*
> *Corpora disponens, mentem non vidit in arte;*
> *Recta animi primum debuit esse via.*
> [O wretched clay which Prometheus first moulded!
> How unwisely he wrought! By his art he arranged the
> body but saw not the mind. The right way would have
> been to start off with the soul.]

– On Restraining Your Will –

C ompared with the common run of men, few
things touch me or, to speak more correctly, get a
hold on me (it being reasonable for things to touch us
provided that they do not take us over). I exercise great
care to extend by reason and reflection this privileged
lack of emotion, which is by nature well advanced in
me. I am wedded to few things and so am passionate
about few. My sight is clear but I fix it on only a few
objectives; my perception is scrupulous and receptive,
but I find things hard to grasp and my concentration
is vague. I do not easily get involved. As far as possible
I work entirely on my self, but even on that subject I
prefer to rein back my emotion so as to stop it from
plunging right in, since it is a subject which I possess
at the mercy of Another – Fortune having more rights
over it than I do.

I value health most highly: but it follows that I
ought not to seek or desire even that so frenetically
that I find illness unbearable. We should follow the
Mean between hatred of pain and love of pleasure:
Plato prescribes a way of life midway between the two.
But there are emotions which drag me from myself and
tie me up elsewhere: those I oppose with all my might.

In my opinion we must lend ourselves to others but give ourselves to ourselves alone. Even if my will did find it easy to pawn and bind itself to others, I could not persevere: by nature and habit I am too fastidious for that:

> *fugax rerum, securaque in otia natus.*
> [fleeing from obligations and born for untroubled leisure.]

Stubborn earnest arguments which ended in victory for my opponent, as well as results which made me ashamed of my hot pursuit, might indeed most cruelly gnaw at me. If I were to then bite back as others do my soul would never find the strength to support the alarms and commotions which attend those who embrace so much: it would straightway be put out of joint by such internal strife. If I am occasionally pressed into taking in hand some business foreign to me, then it is in hand that I promise to take it, not in lung nor in liver! I accept the burdens but I refuse to make them parts of my body. Take trouble over them: yes; get worked up about them: never. I look after them, but not like a broody hen. I have enough to do to order and arrange those pressing affairs of my own which lie within my veins and vitals without having a jostling crowd of other folk's affairs lodged there and trampling all over me; I have enough to do to attend to matters which by nature belong to my own being without inviting in outsiders. Those who realise what they owe to themselves, and the great duties which bind themselves to themselves, discover that Nature has made that an ample enough charge and by no means a sinecure. Do not go far away: you have plenty to do 'at home!' Men put themselves up for hire. Their talents are not for themselves but for those to whom they have enslaved themselves. They are never 'at home': their tenants are there! That widespread attitude does not please me. We should husband our soul's freedom, never pawning it, save on occasions when it is proper to do so – which, if we judge soundly, are very few.

Just watch people who have been conditioned to let themselves be enraptured and carried away: they do it all the time, in small matters as in great, over things which touch them and those which touch them not at all. They become involved, indiscriminately, wherever there is a task and obligations; they are not alive without bustle and bother. '*in negotiis sunt negotii causa*'. [They are busy so as to *be* busy.] The only reason why they seek occupations is to be occupied. It is not a case of wanting to move but of being unable to hold still, just as a rock shaken loose cannot arrest its fall until it lies on the bottom. For a certain type of man, being busy is a mark of competence and dignity. Their minds seek repose in motion, like babes in a cradle. They can say that they are as useful to their friends as they are bothersome to themselves. Nobody gives his money away to others: everyone gives his time. We are never more profligate than with the very things over which avarice would be useful and laudable.

The complexion which I adopt is flat contrary to that. I keep within myself; such things as I do want I usually want mildly. And I want very few. I rarely become involved in anything; if I am busy I am calmly so. What others want or do, they want with all their will, frantically. There are so many awkward passages that the surest way is to glide rather lightly over the surface of this world. We should slide over it, not get bogged down in it. Pleasure itself is painful in its deeper reaches:

> *incedis per ignes*
> *Suppositos cineri doloso*
> [You are walking through fires hidden beneath
> treacherous ashes.]

The Jurors of Bordeaux elected me mayor of their city when I was far from France, and even farther from such a thought. I declined; but I was brought to see that I was wrong, since the King had also interposed his command.

It is an office which should seem all the more splendid for having no salary or reward other than the honour of doing it. It lasts two years, but can be extended by a second election. That very rarely happens. It did in my case; and to two others previously: some years ago to Monsieur de Lanssac and more recently to

Monsieur de Biron, Marshal of France, to whose place I succeeded. My own place I yielded to another Marshal of France, Monsieur de Matignon, taking pride in such noble company:

uterque bonus pads bellique minister.
[both good officers in peace and war.]

By those particular circumstances which she contributed herself, Fortune decided to play a part in my preferment. Nor was it entirely vain, since Alexander showed contempt for the ambassadors of Corinth who offered him the citizenship of their city, but when they happened to explain that Bacchus and Hercules were also on the roll of honour he accepted it graciously.

As soon as I arrived I spelled out my character faithfully and truly, just as I know myself to be – no memory, no concentration, no experience, no drive; no hatred either, no ambition, no covetousness, no ferocity – so that they should be told, and therefore know, what to expect from my service. And since the only thing which had spurred them to elect me was what they knew of my father and his honoured memory, I very clearly added that I would be most distressed if anything whatsoever were to make such inroads upon my will as the affairs of their city had made on my father's while he was governing it in the very same situation to which I had been summoned. I can remember seeing him when I was a boy: an old man, cruelly troubled by the worries of office, forgetting the gentle atmosphere of his home (to which he had long been confined by the weakness of advancing years) as well as his estates and his health, thinking little of his own life (which he nearly lost, having been involved for them in long and arduous journeys). That was the kind of man he was: and his character arose from great natural goodness. Never was there a soul of man more charitable, more devoted to the people.

Such ways I praise in others: but do not like to follow them myself: not without some justification. He had heard it said that one should forget oneself on behalf of one's neighbour and that, compared to the general, the individual is of no importance.

Most of the world's rules and precepts do adopt such an attitude, driving us outside ourselves and hounding us into the forum in the interests of the public weal. They thought they were doing some fair deed by diverting us and withdrawing us from ourselves, taking it for granted that we were clinging too much to ourselves by a bond which was all too natural. And they left nothing to that purpose unsaid. It is no novelty that clever men should preach not things as they are but things such as might serve them. Truth has its difficulties, its awkwardnesses and its incompatibilities with us. It is often necessary to deceive us so as to stop us from deceiving ourselves, hooding our eyes and dazzling our minds so as to train them and cure them. '*Imperiti enim judicant, et qui frequenter in hoc ipsum fallendi sunt, ne errent.'* [Those who judge are inexperienced: they must needs be deceived precisely to stop them from going wrong.] When they tell us to prefer to ourselves three, four or fifty categories of objects, they are imitating the art of the bowman, who, so as to hit his target, raises his sights way above it. To straighten a piece of bent wood we bend it right over backwards.

I reckon that in the temple of Pallas (as can be seen to be the case in all other religions) there were open secrets, to be revealed to the people, and other hidden higher ones, to be revealed only to initiates. It is likely that the true degree of love which each man owes to himself is found among the latter: not a false love which makes us embrace glory, knowledge, riches and such-like with an immoderate primary passion, as though they were members of our being, nor a love which is easy-going and random, acting like ivy which cracks and destroys the wall which it clings to, but a healthy, measured love, as useful as it is pleasant. Whoever knows its duties and practises them is truly in the treasure-house of the Muses: he has reached the pinnacle of human happiness and of man's joy. Such a man, knowing precisely what is due to himself, finds that his role includes frequenting men and the world; to do this he must contribute to society the offices and duties which concern him. He who does not live a little for others hardly lives at all for himself: *'Qui sibi amicus est, scito hunc amicum omnibus esse.'* [Know that a man who feels loving-friendship for himself does so for all men.] The chief charge laid upon each one of us is his own conduct: that is why we are here. For example, any man who forgot to live a good and holy life himself, but who thought that he had fulfilled his duties by guiding and training others to do so, would be stupid: in exactly the same way, any man who gives up a sane and happy life in order to provide one for others makes (in my opinion) a bad and unnatural decision.

I have no wish that anyone should refuse to his tasks, when the need arises, his attention, his deeds, his words, or his sweat and blood:

> *non ipse pro charts amicis*
> *Aut patria timidus perire.*
> [personally I am not afraid of dying for those whom I love dearly or for my country.]

But it will be in the form of an incidental loan, his mind meanwhile remaining quiet and sane – not without activity but without distress, without passion. Straightforward action costs him so little that he can do it in his sleep. But it must be set in motion with discernment, for whereas the body accepts whatsoever is loaded upon it according to its real weight the mind expands it and makes it heavier, often to its own cost, giving it whatever dimensions it thinks fit. With different efforts and different straining of our wills we achieve similar things. One thing does not imply the other: for how many soldiers put themselves at risk every day in wars which they care little about, rushing into danger in battles the loss of which will not make them lose a night's sleep: meanwhile another man in his own home and far from that danger (which he would never have dared to face) is more passionate about the outcome of the war, and has his soul in greater travail over it, than the soldier who is shedding his life-blood there. I have been able to engage in public duties without going even a nail's breadth from myself, and to give myself to others without taking myself away from *me*.

Such a rough and violent desire is more of a hindrance than a help in carrying out our projects; it fills us with exasperation in the face of results which are slow to come or which turn against us, and with bitterness and suspicion towards those with whom we are negotiating. We can never control well any business which obsesses and controls us:

> *male cuncta ministrat*
> *Impetus.*
> [violent impulses serve everything badly.]

Anyone who brings only his judgement and talents to the task sets about it more joyfully; totally at his ease, he feints, parries or plays for time as need arises; he can fail to strike home without torment or affliction, ready and intact for a fresh encounter; when he walks he always retains the bridle in his hands. In a man who is bemused by violent and tyrannical strain there can, of necessity, be seen a great deal of unwisdom and injudiciousness. The impetus of his desire carries him along: such a motion is rash and (unless Fortune contributes much) is hardly fruitful. When we punish any injuries which we have received, philosophy wants us to avoid choler, not so as to diminish our revenge but (on the contrary) so that its blows may be weightier and better aimed: philosophy considers violent emotion to be an impediment to that. Choler does not simply confuse: of itself it tires the arms of those who inflict chastisement; its flames confound and exhaust their strength. When you are in a dashing hurry, '*festinatio tarda est*' [haste causes delay]. Haste trips over its own feet, tangles itself up and comes to a halt. '*Ipsa se velocitas implicat.*' [The very haste ties you in knots.] For example, from what I can see to be usually the case, covetousness knows no greater hindrance than itself: the more tense and vigorous it is, the less productive it is. It commonly snaps up riches more quickly when masked by some semblance of generosity.

A gentleman, an excellent fellow and one of my friends, nearly drove himself out of his mind by too much strain and passionate concern for the affairs of a prince, his master: yet that self-same master described himself to me as one who can see the weight of a setback as well as anyone else but who resolves to put up with it whenever there is no remedy; in other cases he orders all the necessary measures to be taken (which he can do promptly because of his quick intelligence) then quietly waits for the outcome. And indeed I have seen him doing it, remaining very cool in his actions and relaxed in his expression throughout some important and ticklish engagements. I find him greater and more able in ill fortune than in good; his defeats are more glorious to him than his victories: his mortifications more glorious than his triumphs.

Consider how even in vain and trivial pursuits such as chess or tennis matches, the keen and burning involvement of a rash desire at once throws your mind into a lack of discernment and your limbs into confusion: you daze yourself and tangle yourself up. A man who reacts with greater moderation towards winning or losing is always 'at home': the less he goads himself on, and the less passionate he is about the game, the more surely and successfully he plays it.

Moreover we impede our soul's grip and her grasp by giving her too much to embrace. Some things should be merely shown to her; some affixed to her and others incorporated into her. The soul can see and know all things, but she should feed only on herself; she should be taught what properly concerns her, what goods and substances are properly hers. The Laws of Nature teach us what our just needs are. The wise first tell us that no man is poor by Nature's standards and that, by opinion's standards, every man is; they then finely distinguish between desires coming from Nature and those coming from the unruliness of our thoughts:

those whose limits we can see are hers; those which flee before us and whose end we can never reach are our own. To cure poverty of possessions is easy: poverty of soul, impossible.

> *Nam si, quod satis est homini, id satis esse potesset,*
> *Hoc sat erat: nunc, cum hoc non est, qui credimus porro*
> *Divitias ullas animum mi explere potese?*
> [This would be enough, if enough could really be enough for any man. Since it never is, why should we believe that any wealth can glut my mind?]

When Socrates saw a great quantity of wealth (valuable jewels and ornaments) being borne in procession through the city, he exclaimed: 'How many things there which I do not want!' Metrodorus lived on twelve ounces a day; Epicurus on less; Metrocles slept among his sheep in the winter and, in summer, in the temple porticos; '*Sufficit ad id natura, quod poscit.*' [What nature demands, she supplies.] Cleanthes lived by his hands and boasted that 'Cleanthes, if he so wished, could support another Cleanthes.'

If what Nature precisely and basically requires for the preservation of our being is too little (and how little it is and how cheaply life can be sustained cannot be better expressed than by the following consideration: that it is so little that it escapes the grasp and blows of Fortune) then let us allow ourselves to take a little more: let us still call 'nature' the habits and endowments of

each one of us; let us appraise ourselves and treat ourselves by that measure: let us stretch our appurtenanc-
es and our calculations as far as that. For as far as that,
it does seem that we have a good excuse: custom is a
second nature and no less powerful; if I lack anything
which I have become used to, I hold that I truly lack
it. I would just as soon (almost) that you took my life
than have you restrict it or lop it much below the state
in which I have lived it for so long. I am not suited
any more to great changes nor to throwing myself into
some new and unaccustomed way of life – not even a
richer one. It is no longer the time to become different.
And if some great stroke of luck should fall into my
hands now, how sorry I would be that it did not come
when I could have enjoyed it.

> *Quo mihi fortuna, si non conceditur uti?*
> [What is a fortune to me if I am not able to use it?]

I would similarly regret any new inward attain-
ment. It is almost better never to become a good man
at all than to do so tardily, understanding how to live
when you have no life ahead. I am on the way out: I
would readily leave to one who comes later whatever
wisdom I am learning about dealing with the world.
I do not want even a good thing when it is too late to
use it. Mustard after dinner! What use is knowledge
to a man with no brain left? It is an insult and dis-
favour of Fortune to offer us presents which fill us with

just indignation because they were lacking to us in due season. Take me no farther; I can go on no more. Of all the qualities which sufficiency possesses, endurance alone suffices. Try giving the capabilities of an outstanding treble to a chorister whose lungs are diseased, or eloquence to a hermit banished to the deserts of Arabia! No art is required to decline. At the finish of every task the ending makes itself known. My world is over: my mould has been emptied; I belong entirely to the past; I am bound to acknowledge that and to conform my exit to it. This I will say to explain what I mean: the recent suppression of ten days by the Pope has brought me so low that I really cannot bear it: I belong to those years when we computed otherwise: so ancient and long-established a custom claims me and summons me back to it. Since I cannot stand novelty even when corrective, I am constrained to be a bit of a heretic in this case. I grit my teeth, but my mind is always ten days ahead or ten days behind; it keeps muttering in my ears: 'That adjustment concerns those not yet born.'

Although health – oh so sweet! – comes and finds me spasmodically, it is so as to bring me nostalgia, not right of possession. I no longer have anywhere to put it. Time is quitting me: without time there is no right of possession. What little value would I attribute to those great elective offices-of-state which are bestowed only on those who are on the way out! No one is concerned there with whether you will perform them properly but how short a time you have to fill them. From the moment of your entry they are thinking of your exit.

Here, I am in short putting the finishing touches to a particular man, not making another one instead. By long accustoming this form of mine has passed into substance and my fortune into nature. So I maintain that each wretched one of us may be pardoned for reckoning as his whatever is comprised within the measure of custom, and also that, beyond those limits, there is nought but confusion. It is the widest extent that we can allow to our rights: the more we increase our needs and possessions the more we expose ourselves to adversities and to the blows of Fortune. The course run by our desires must be circumscribed and restricted to the narrow limits of the most accessible and contiguous pleasures. Moreover their course should be set not in a straight line terminating somewhere else but in a circle both the start and finish of which remain and terminate within ourselves after a short gallop round: any action carried through without such a return on itself – and I mean a quick and genuine one – is wayward and diseased: such are those of covetous and ambitious men and of so many others who dash towards a goal, careering ever on and on.

Most of our occupations are farcical: '*Mundus universus exercet histrionem.*' [Everybody in the entire world is acting a part.] We should play our role properly, but as the role of a character which we have adopted. We must not turn masks and semblances into essential realities, nor adopted qualities into attributes of our self. We cannot tell our skin from our shimmy! It is enough to plaster flour on our faces without doing it to our minds. I know some who transubstantiate and metamorphose themselves into as many new beings and forms as the dignities which they assume: they are prelates down to their guts and livers and uphold their offices on their lavatory-seat. I cannot make them see the difference between hats doffed to them and those doffed to their commissions, their retinue or their mule. '*Tantum se fortunae permittunt, etiam ut naturam dediscant.*' [They allow so much to their Fortune that they unlearn their own natures.] They puff up their souls and inflate their natural speech to the height of the magistrate's bench.

The Mayor and Montaigne have always been twain, very clearly distinguished. Just because you are a lawyer or a financier you must not ignore the trickery there is in such vocations: a man of honour is not accountable for the crimes or stupidities of his profession, nor should they make him refuse to practise it; such is the custom of his country: and he gets something from it. We must make our living from the world and use it as it is. Yet even an Emperor's judgement should be above his imperial sway, seeing it and thinking of it as an extraneous accessory. He should know how to enjoy himself independently of it, talking (at least to himself) as Tom, Dick or Harry.

I cannot get so deeply and totally involved. When

my convictions make me devoted to one faction, it is not with so violent a bond that my understanding becomes infected by it. During the present confusion in this State of ours my own interest has not made me fail to recognise laudable qualities in our adversaries nor reprehensible ones among those whom I follow. People worship everything on their own side: for most of what I see on mine I do not even make excuses. A good book does not lose its beauty because it argues against my cause. Apart from the kernel of the controversy, I have remained balanced and utterly indifferent: '*Neque extra necessitates belli praecipuum odium gero.*' [And I act with no special hatred beyond what war requires.] I congratulate myself for that: it is usual to fall into the opposite extreme: '*Utatur motu animi qui uti ratione non potest*' [If he cannot be reasonable, let him indulge his emotions!]

Those who extend their anger and hatred beyond their concerns (as most men do) betray that their emotion arises from something else, from some private cause, just as when a man is cured of his ulcer but still has a fever that shows that it arises from some other and more secret origin. The fact is that they feel no anger at all for the general cause in so far as it inflicts wounds on the interests of all men and on the State: they resent it simply because it bruises their private interest. That is why they goad themselves into a private passion which goes beyond public justice and reason: '*Nam tarn omnia universi quam ea quae ad quemque per-*

tinent singuli carpebant.' [They did not carp about the terms as a whole but about how they affected them as individuals.]

I want us to win, but I am not driven mad if we do not. I am firmly attached to the sanest of the parties, but I do not desire to be particularly known as an enemy of the others beyond what is generally reasonable. I absolutely condemn such defective arguments as, 'He belongs to the League because he admires the grace of Monsieur de Guise'; 'He is. Huguenot: the activity of the King of Navarre sends him into ecstasies'; 'He finds such-and-such lacking in the manners of the King: at heart he is a traitor.' I did not concede to the magistrate himself that he was right to condemn a book for having named a heretic among the best poets of the age. Should we be afraid to say that a thief has nice shins! Must a whore smell horrid? In wiser ages did they revoke Marcus Manlius' proud title *Capitolinus*, awarded him earlier as saviour of the liberty and religion of the State? Did they smother the memory of his generosity, of his feats of arms and the military honours awarded for his valour, because he subsequently hankered after kingship, to the prejudice of the laws of his land?

Some start hating a barrister: by next morning they are saying that he is a poor speaker! (I have touched elsewhere on how zeal has driven decent men to similar errors. For my part I can easily say, 'He does this wickedly, that virtuously.') Similarly, when the outlook

or the outcome of an event is unfavourable, they want
each man to be blind and insensible towards his own
party, and that our judgement and conviction should
serve not the truth but to project our desires. I would
rather err to the other extreme, for I fear that my desires may seduce me. Added to which I have a rather
delicate mistrust of anything I desire. I have seen in
my time amazing examples of the indiscriminate and
prodigious facility which peoples have for letting their
beliefs be led and their hopes be manipulated towards
what has pleased and served their leaders, despite dozens of mistakes piled one upon another and despite
illusions and deceptions. I am no longer struck with
wonder at those who were led by the nose by the apish
miracles of Apollonius and Mahomet: their thoughts
and their minds had been stifled by their emotions.
Their power of discernment could no longer admit anything save that which smiled upon them and favoured
their cause.

I thought this had attained its highest degree in
the first of our feverish factions: that other one, born
subsequently, imitated it and surpasses it. From which
I conclude that it is a quality inseparable from mass
aberrations: all opinions tumble out after the first one,
whipped along like waves in the wind. You do not belong if you can change your mind, if you do not bob
along with all the rest. Yet we certainly do wrong to
just parties when we would support them by trickery. I
have always opposed that. It only works for sick minds:

for sane ones there are surer ways (not merely more honourable ones) of sustaining courage and explaining setbacks.

The heavens have never seen strife as grievous as that between Caesar and Pompey, and never will again. Yet I believe I can detect in both their fair, noble souls a great moderation towards each other. Their rivalry over honour and command did not sweep them into frenzied and indiscriminate hatred. Even in their harshest deeds I can discover some remnants of respect and good-will, which leads me to conclude that, had it been possible, each of them would have wished to achieve his ends without the downfall of his fellow rather than with it.

Between Marius and Sylla how different things were! Take warning. We should not dash so madly after our emotions and selfish interests. When I was young I resisted the advances of love as soon as I realised that it was getting too much hold over me; I took care that it was not so delightful to me that it finally took me by storm and held me captive entirely at its mercy: on all the other occasions upon which my will seizes too avidly I do the same: I lean in the opposite direction when I see it leaping in and wallowing in its own wine; I avoid so far fuelling the advance of its pleasure that I cannot retake it without loss and bloodshed.

There are souls which, through insensitivity, see only half of anything; they enjoy the good fortune of being less bruised by harmful events. That is a leprosy

of the mind which has some appearance of sanity –
and of such a sanity as philosophy does not entirely despise; for all that, it is not reasonable to call it wisdom,
as we often do. There was a man in antiquity who for
just such an affectation mocked Diogenes who, to assay his powers of endurance, went out stark naked and
threw his arms round a snowman. He came across him
in that attitude. 'Feeling very cold just now?' he asked.
'Absolutely not,' replied Diogenes. 'In that case,' con-
tinued the other, 'what is there hard and exemplary, do
you think, about hanging on out there?'

To measure steadfastness we must know what is
suffered. But let those souls which have to experience
the adversities and injuries of Fortune in all their depth
and harshness and which have to weigh them at their
natural weight and taste them according to their natural bitterness employ their arts to avoid being involved
in what causes them and to deflect their approaches.
What was it that King Cotys did? He paid handsomely
when some beautiful and ornate tableware was offered
to him, but since it was unusually fragile he immediately smashed the lot, ridding himself in time of an easy
occasion for anger against his servants.

I have likewise deliberately avoided confusion of
interests; I have not sought properties adjoining those
of close relatives or belonging to folk to whom I should
be linked by close affection; from thence arise estrange-
ments and dissension.

I used to like games of chance with cards and dice.

I rid myself of them long ago – for one reason only: whenever I lost, no matter what a good face I put on, I still felt a stab of pain. A man of honour, who must take it deeply to heart if he is insulted or given the lie and not be one to accept some nonsense to pay and console him for his loss, should avoid letting controversies grow as well as stubborn quarrels. I avoid like the plague morose men of gloomy complexions, and I do not engage in any discussions which I cannot treat without self-interest or emotion, unless compelled to do so by duty: *'Melius non incipient, quam desinent.'* [Better that they should never begin than to leave off.] The safest way is to be prepared before the event. I am well aware that there have been sages who have adopted a different course: they were not afraid to sink their hooks deep, engaging themselves in several objectives. Those fellows are sure of their fortitude, beneath which they can shelter against all kinds of hostile events, wrestling against evils by the power of their endurance:

> *velut rupes vastum quæ prodit in æquor,*
> *Obvia ventorum furiis, expostaque ponto,*
> *Vim cunctam atque minas perfert cœlique marisque,*
> *Ipsa immota manens.*
> [as a cliff, jutting out into the vast expanse of ocean,
> exposed to furious winds and confronting the waves,
> braves the menaces of sea and sky and itself remains
> unmoved.]

Let us not attempt to follow such examples: we shall never manage it. Such men have made up their minds to watch resolutely and unmoved the destruction of their country, which once held and governed all their affection. For common souls like ours there is too much strain, too much savagery in that. Cato gave up for his country the most noble life there ever was; little men like us should flee farther from the storm; we should see that there are no pains to feel, no pains to endure, dodging blows not parrying them. When Zeno saw Chremonides, a young man whom he loved, coming to sit beside him, he jumped up. Cleanthes asked why. 'I understand,' he replied, 'that when any part of the body starts to swell the doctors chiefly prescribe rest and forbid emotion.' Socrates never says, 'Do not surrender to the attraction of beauty; resist it; struggle against it.' He says, 'Flee it; run from its sight and from any encounter with it, as from a potent poison which can dart and strike you from afar.' And that good disciple of his, describing either fictionally or historically (though in my opinion more historically than fictionally) the rare perfections of Cyrus the Great, shows him distrusting his ability to resist the attractions of the heavenly beauty of his captive the illustrious Panthea: it was to a man who was less at liberty than he was that he gave the tasks of visiting her and guarding her. And the Holy Ghost likewise says, '*Ne nos inducas in tentationem.*' [Lead us not into temptation.] We pray, not that our reason may not be assailed and overcome by worldly desires, but that it may not even be assayed by them, that we be not led into a position where we have even merely to withstand the approaches, blandishments and temptations of sin, and we beseech our Lord to keep our consciences quiet, wholly and completely delivered from commerce with evil.

Those who say that they have got the better of their vindictive feelings or of some other species of blameworthy passion often speak truly of things as they are but not as they were. They are talking to us now that the causes behind their error have been advanced and promoted by themselves. But push farther back; summon those causes back to their first principles: there you will catch them napping. Do they expect their faults to be trivial just because they are older, and that the outcome of an unjust beginning should be just?

Whoever would wish his country well (as I do) without getting ulcers about it or wasting away will, when he sees it threatening either to collapse in ruin or to continue in a no-less-ruinous state, be unhappy about it but not knocked senseless. O wretched ship of State, 'hauled in different direction by the waves, the winds and the man at the wheel':

> *in tam diversa magister,*
> *Ventus et unda trahunt.*

Whoever does not gape after the favours of princes as something he cannot live without is not greatly stung by the coldness of their reception nor the fickleness of their wills. A man who does not brood over his children or his honours with slavish propensity does not cease to live comfortably after he has lost them. Whoever acts well mainly for his own satisfaction is not much put out when he sees men judging his deeds contrary to his merit. A quarter of an ounce of endurance can provide for such discomforts. I find that the remedy which works for me is, from the outset, to purchase my freedom at the cheapest price I can get; I know that I have by this means escaped much travail and hardship. With very little effort I stop the first movement of my emotions, giving up whatever begins to weigh on me before it bears me off. If you do not stop the start, you will never stop the race. If you cannot slam the door against your emotions you will never chase them out once they have got in. If you cannot struggle through the beginning, you will never get through the end; nor will you withstand the building's fall, if you cannot stand its being shaken. '*Etenim ipsæ se impellunt ubi semel a ratione discessum est; ipsaque sibi imbecillitas indulget, in altutnque provehitur imprudens, nec repent locum consistendi.*' [Once they have departed from reason the emotions drive themselves on; their very weakness indulges itself, venturing imprudently on to the deep and finding no place in which it can heave to.]

I can feel in time the tiny breezes which come fondling me and rustling within me, as forerunners of

gales: '*Animus, multo antequam opprimatur, quatitur.*'
[The mind is lashed well before it is engulfed.]

> *Ceu flamina prima*
> *Cum deprensa fremunt sylvis, et cœca volutant*
> *Murmura, venturos nautis prodentia ventos.*
> [Thus when the light breeze is pent up in the wood-
> lands, it swirls about and makes a sullen roar, warning
> seamen that a storm is nigh.]

How frequently have I done myself an evident injustice so as to avoid the risk of receiving a worse one
from the judges after years of agony and of vile and base
machinations which are more hostile to my nature than
the rack or pyre. '*Convenit a litibus quantum licet, et
nescio an paulo plus etiam quam licet, abhorrentem esse.
Est enim non modo liberale, paululum nonnunquam de
suo jure decedere, sed interdum etiam fructuosum.*' [It is
seemly to avoid lawsuits as far as you should, and even
a little bit further. It is not only gentlemanly to waive
one's rights a little it is sometimes also profitable.] If
we were truly wise we should delight in it and boast
about it, like the innocent son of a great house whom
I heard happily welcoming each guest with, 'Mother
has just lost her case!' as though her case were a cough
or a fever or some other thing which it is grievous to
have. Even such advantages as Fortune has favoured
me with – namely kinships and ties with men who have
supreme authority over matters of that kind – I have

consciously striven hard to avoid exploiting to the detriment of anyone else or to inflate my rights beyond their rightful worth. In short I am happy to say that I have spent all my days virgin of lawsuits (even though they have not failed frequently to offer themselves to my service on many a just pretext if only I would listen) and virgin of actions against me. So I shall soon have spent a long life without serious harm given or received, and without being called anything worse than my name: a rare gift of Heaven.

Our greatest commotions arise from laughable principles and causes. What ruin befell our last Duke of Burgundy because of an action against him for a cartload of sheep-skins. And was not the engraving on a seal the original and main cause of the most horrifying disaster that the fabric of this world has ever suffered? (For Pompey and Caesar are only side-shoots, consequent upon the first two rivals.) And in my own day I have seen the wisest heads in this Kingdom assembled with great ceremony and at great public expense to make treaties and agreements, while the details of them depended on sovereign chatter in the ladies' drawing-room and on the inclination of some slip of a woman. The poets understood that rightly enough when they put all Greece and Asia to fire and bloody strife for the sake of an apple.

Think why that man over there takes his sword and dagger and risks his life and honour; let him tell you the source of the quarrel: the occasion was so trivial that he cannot tell you of it without blushing. When it is starting to ferment, all you need is a little wisdom. Once you have embarked, all the hawsers pull tight: then, great precautions are needed, much more difficult and important ones.

How much easier it is never to get in than to get yourself out! We should act contrary to the reed which, when it first appears, throws up a long straight stem but afterwards, as though it were exhausted and had lost its wind, makes several dense nodules, as so many respites which indicate that it no longer has its original vigour and drive. We must rather begin gently and coolly, saving our breath for the encounter and our vigorous thrusts for finishing the job off. In their beginnings it is we who guide affairs and hold them in our power; but once they are set in motion, it is they which guide us and sweep us along and we who have to follow.

Yet that does not mean that this stratagem of mine has relieved me of all difficulties or that I have not often found it very hard to master or bridle my emotions. They cannot always be restrained to the measure of their causes, and even their beginnings can be harsh and aggressive. Nevertheless there are fair savings to be derived from it, and some fruits too except by those whom no fruit can satisfy when no honour is to be had. For in truth such an action can only be valued by each man himself. You yourself are happier but you are not more esteemed, since you reformed yourself before you took to the floor, before the matter could be seen. However there is this as well: not merely in this case but in all other of life's duties, the way of those who aim at honour is different indeed from that followed by those whose objective is the ordinate and reasonable.

I find that some dash thoughtlessly and furiously into the lists only to slow down during the charge. Plutarch says that those who suffer from excessive diffidence readily and easily agree to anything but also readily break their word and go back on what they have said; so, similarly, anyone who enters lightly upon a quarrel is liable to be equally light in getting out of it. The same difficulty which stops me from broaching anything would spur me on once I was heated and excited. What a bad way to do it: once you are in, you must go on or burst! 'Undertake relaxedly,' said Bias, 'but pursue hotly.'

But what is even less tolerable, for want of wisdom we decline into want of bravery.

Today most settlements of our disputes are shameful and lying: we merely seek to save appearances, while betraying and disowning our true thoughts. We plaster over facts; we know how we said it and what we meant by it; the bystanders know it; so do our friends to whom we wished to prove our superiority. We disavow our thoughts at the expense of our frankness and our reputation for courage, seeking bolt-holes in falsehoods so as to reach a conciliation. We give the lie to ourselves in order to get out the fact that we gave the lie to somebody else. You ought not to be considering whether your gesture or words may be given a different meaning: from now on it is your true and honest meaning that you should be seeking to defend, no matter what the cost. At stake are your morality and your honour: those are not qualities for you to protect behind a mask. Let us leave such servile shifts and expediences to the chicanery of the law-courts. Every day I see excuses and reparations made to purge an indiscretion which seem uglier to me than the indiscretion itself. It would be better to offend your adversary afresh than to commit an offence against yourself by making him such a reparation as that. You were moved to anger when you defied him: now that you are cooler and more sensible, you are going to appease him and fawn on him! That way, you retreat further than you ever advanced. I reckon that nothing which a gentleman says can seem worse than the shame of his unsaying it under duress from authority: stubbornness in a gentleman is more pardonable than pusillanimity.

For me passions are as easy to avoid as hard to moderate: '*Abscinduntur facilius animo quam temperantur.*' [They are more easily cut out from the mind than tempered.]

If a man cannot attain to that noble Stoic impassibility, let him hide in the lap of this peasant insensitivity of mine. What Stoics did from virtue I teach myself to do from temperament. Storms lodge in the middle regions; philosophers and country bumpkins – the two extremes – meet in peace of mind and happiness.

> *Fœlix qui potuit rerum cognoscere causas,*
> *Atque metus omnes et inexorabile fatum*
> *Subjecit pedibus, strepitumque Acherontis avari.*
> *Fortunatus et ille Deos qui novit agrestes,*
> *Panaque, sylvanumque senem, nymphasque sorores.*
> [Blessed the man who can find out causes, who can trample down all fears of inexorable Fate and the howls of the close-fisted Underworld: blessed, too, he who knows the rustic gods, Pan, old Sylvanus and the sister nymphs.]

The infancies of all things are feeble and weak. We must keep our eyes open at their beginnings; you cannot find the danger then because it is so small: once it has grown, you cannot find the cure. While chasing ambition I would have had to face, every day, thousands of irritations harder to digest than the difficulty I had in putting a stop to my natural inclination towards it.

> *jure perhorrui*
> *Late conspicuum tollere verticem.*
> [I was right to abhor raising my head and attracting attention.]

All public deeds are liable to ambiguous and diverse interpretations since so many heads are judging them. Now about this municipal office of mine (and I am delighted to say a word about it, not that it is worth it but to show how I behave in such matters): some say that I bore myself as a man who shows too little passion and whose zeal was too slack. As far as appearances go, they were not all that wrong: I assay keeping my soul and my thoughts in repose: '*Cum semper natura, tum etiam aetate jam quietus*' [Always tranquil by nature, I now am also so by my age]; if they turn riotous from some deep and disturbing impression that, in truth, is against my intention. Yet from this natural languor of mine one should not draw evidence of incapacity (since lack of worry and lack of wit are two different things) and even less of ingratitude or of lack of appreciation towards those citizens who went to every available extreme to please me, both before and after they knew me – for they did far more for me in re-electing me to office than in electing me in the first place. I wish them all possible good: and indeed, if the occasion had arisen, there is nothing that I would have spared in their service. I bestirred myself as much for them as I do for myself. They are a fine people, good brave fighting-men, able therefore to accept discipline and obedience and to serve a good cause when well led.

People also say that my period of office passed without trace or mark. Good. They accuse me of being dilatory at a time when nearly everyone else was convicted of doing too much. I paw the ground when my will bolts away with me: but that trait is the enemy of perseverance. Should anyone wish to use me as I am, let him give me tasks which require vigour and frankness, as well as straightforward, brief and hazardous execution. I could do something then. But if it needs to be subtle, toilsome, clever and tortuous, better ask somebody else.

Not all important commissions are difficult. I would have been prepared to work a little harder had that been very necessary: I am capable of doing somewhat more than I do or like to do. To the best of my knowledge I never left undone any action that duty seriously required of me; but I readily overlooked those where ambition mingles with duty and uses it as a pretext it is those which, more often than not, fill men's eyes and ears and please them; they are satisfied not with realities but appearances. If they do not hear a sound they think you are asleep! My own humours are opposed to noisy ones: I could certainly remain undisturbed while quelling a disturbance, and could punish a riot without losing my temper. Should I need a little choler and fire, then I borrow some to mask me. My manners are unabrasive, more insipid than sharp: I do not bring actions against an official who dozes, provided that those whom he administers can doze quietly with him. That is the way the laws doze.

Personally I favour an obscure mute life which slips by: '*neque submissam et abjectam, neque se efferentem*' [neither submissive and mean nor puffed up]. That is how my Fortune wills it: I was born into a family which has flowed on without brilliance or turbulence, one long remembered as being particularly ambitious for probity. Nowadays men are so conditioned to bustle and ostentation that we have lost the feel of goodness, moderation, even-temper, steadfastness and other such quiet and unpretentious qualities; rough objects make themselves felt: smooth ones can be handled without sensation. Illness is felt: good health, little or not at all; neither do we feel things which flatter us, compared with those which batter us.

If we postpone something which could be done in the council-chamber until it is done in the market-square, keeping back till noon something which could have been finished the night before, or if we are anxious to do personally something which a colleague could have done just as well, then we are acting for the sake of our own reputation and for private advantage, not for the Good. (That is what some barber-surgeons used to do in ancient Greece, performing their operations on a daïs in view of passers-by so as to enlarge their practices and the number of patients.) They think that good regulations can only be heard when announced with a fanfare.

Ambition is not a vice fit for little fellows or for enterprises such as ours. Alexander was told: 'Your father will leave you wide dominions, peaceful and secure.' But that lad wanted to rival his father's victorious and righteous government. He had no wish to enjoy ruling the entire world undemandingly and peacefully. (Alcibiades in Plato says he prefers to die young as a beautiful, rich, noble and exceedingly learned youth than to stay fixed in those qualities.)

Ambition is doubtless a pardonable malady in a strong and full soul such as Alexander's. But when petty, dwarfish souls start aping them, believing that they can scatter their renown abroad by having judged one matter rightly or for having arranged the changing of the guard at the town gate, then the higher they hope to raise their heads the more they bare their arses. Such petty achievements have no body, no life; they start evaporating on the first man's lips and never get from one street-corner to another. Have the effrontery to talk about them to your son or your man-servant, like that old fellow who had nobody else to listen to his praises or to acknowledge his worth and so boasted to his chambermaid: 'Oh, what a gallant and clever man you have for a master, Perrette!' If the worse comes to worst, talk about it to yourself, like a King's Counsel I know who, having (with extreme exertion and extreme absurdity) disgorged a boatload of legal references, withdrew from the council-chamber to the court piss-house, where he was heard devoutly muttering through his teeth: '*Non nobis, Domine, non nobis, sed nomine tuo da gloriam.*' [Not unto us, O Lord, not unto us, but unto Thy Name be the glory.] If you cannot get it from somebody else's purse, get it from your own!

Fame does not play the whore for so base a price. Those rare and exemplary deeds to which fame is due would not tolerate the company of such a countless mob of petty everyday actions. Marble can boast your titles as much as you like for having repaired a stretch of wall or cleaned up some public gutter, but men of sense will not. Renown does not ensue upon anything done well unless difficulty and unusualness are involved. Indeed, according to the Stoics, simple esteem is not due to every action born of virtue: they would not even faintly praise a man for having abstained from some sore-eyed old whore for temperance' sake! Those who already knew of the astonishing qualities of Scipio Africanus rejected the 'glory' which Panaetius gave him for refusing bribes: that glory was not his alone but belonged to his entire age.

We have pleasures appropriate to our station: let us not usurp those of greatness: ours are more natural and are the more solid and certain for being more humble. Let us reject ambition out of ambition, since we do not do so out of a sense of right and wrong; let us despise that base beggerly hunger for renown and honour which makes us solicit them from all kinds of people by abject means, no matter how vile the price: '*Quae est ista laus quae possit e macello peti?*' [What kind of praise is it that you can order from the butcher's?] To be honoured thus is a dishonour.

Let us learn to be no more avid for glory than we deserve. Boasting of every useful or blameless action is for men in whom such things are rare and unusual: they want them to be valued at what it cost them! The more glittering the deed the more I subtract from its moral worth, because of the suspicion aroused in me that it was exposed more for glitter than for goodness: goods displayed are already half-way to being sold. The most elegant deeds are those which slip from the doer's hand nonchalantly and without fuss, and which some man of honour later picks out and saves from obscurity, bringing them to light for their own sake. '*Mihi quidem laudabiliora videntur omnia, quae sine venditatione et sine populo teste fiunt*' [Personally I always find more praiseworthy whatever is done without ostentation and without public witnesses] – says the vainest man in the world!

I had nothing to do except to preserve things and to keep them going; those are dull and unnoticeable tasks. There is a great deal of splendour in innovation, but that is under a ban nowadays when it is by novelties alone that we are oppressed, against novelties alone that we must defend ourselves. Although it is less in the daylight, refraining from action is often more noble than action: what little I am worth is virtually all on that side. In short, my opportunities while in office accorded with my temperament. I am most grateful to them for it. Is there any man who wants to be ill so as to provide work for his doctor? Ought we not to whip a doctor who hoped for the plague so as to practise his Art? Although that wicked humour is common enough, I have never hoped that trouble and distemper in this city might increase the glory and honour of my mayoralty. I put my shoulder loyally to the wheel to make things smooth and easy.

Even he who would not show me gratitude for the gentle and muted calm which accompanied my administration cannot at least deprive me of that share which does belong to me by title of my good fortune. And I am so made that I would as soon be fortunate as wise, owing my success simply to God's grace rather than to the intervention of my labours. I had proclaimed most eloquently to the whole world my inadequacy for handling such public affairs. And I have something worse than that inadequacy: the fact that I hardly find it displeasing and, given the kind of life that I have sketched out for myself, that I hardly even attempt to cure it.

Now I was not satisfied, either, with my conduct of affairs: but I did achieve – more or less – what I promised myself I would, and I far exceeded what I promised to those whom I was dealing with, since I prefer to promise rather less than I can do and hope to do. I am sure I left no injury or hatred behind me: as for leaving any regret or desire for me, I do at least know that I never much cared for that.

> *Mene huic confidere monstro,*
> *Mene salis placidi vultum fluctusque quietos*
> *Ignorare?*
> [Me! put faith in such a monster! Me! not realise that the sea simply happens to be calm and to look peaceful!]

CLASSIC COLLECTION

The Classic Collection brings together the finest essayists of the past, introduced by contemporary writers.

Grumbling at Large – Selected Essays of J. B. Priestley
Introduced by Valerie Grove

Beautiful and Impossible Things
– Selected Essays of Oscar Wilde
Introduced by Gyles Brandreth

Words of Fire – Selected Essays of Ahad Ha'am
Introduced by Brian Klug

Essays on the Self – Selected Essays of Virginia Woolf
Introduced by Joanna Kavenna

All That is Worth Remembering
– Selected Essays of William Hazlitt
Introduced by Duncan Wu

*All NHE titles are available in the UK, and some titles are available in the rest of the world. For more information, please visit www.nottinghilleditions.com.

A selection of our titles is distributed in the US and Canada by New York Review Books. For more information on available titles, please visit www.nyrb.com.